AYHAN ÇİLİNGİROĞLU

MANUFACTURE OF HEAVY ELECTRICAL EQUIPMENT IN DEVELOPING COUNTRIES

WORLD BANK STAFF OCCASIONAL PAPERS NUMBER NINE

INTERNATIONAL BANK FOR RECONSTRUCTION AND DEVELOPMENT

INTERNATIONAL BANK FOR RECONSTRUCTION AND DEVELOPMENT

WORLD BANK STAFF OCCASIONAL PAPERS NUMBER NINE

AYHAN ÇİLİNGİROĞLU

MANUFACTURE OF HEAVY ELECTRICAL EQUIPMENT IN DEVELOPING COUNTRIES

Distributed by The Johns Hopkins Press
Baltimore and London

FOREWORD

I would like to explain *why* the World Bank Group does research work, and why it publishes it. We feel an obligation to look beyond the projects we help to finance toward the whole resource allocation of an economy, and the effectiveness of the use of those resources. Our major concern, in dealings with member countries, is that all scarce resources, including capital, skilled labor, enterprise and know-how, should be used to their best advantage. We want to see policies that encourage appropriate increases in the supply of savings, whether domestic or international. Finally, we are required by our Articles, as well as by inclination, to use objective economic criteria in all our judgments.

These are our preoccupations, and these, one way or another, are the subjects of most of our research work. Clearly, they are also the proper concern of anyone who is interested in promoting development, and so we seek to make our research papers widely available. In doing so, we have to take the risk of being misunderstood. Although these studies are published by the Bank, the views expressed and the methods explored should not necessarily be considered to represent the Bank's views or policies. Rather they are offered as a modest contribution to the great discussion on how to advance the economic development of the underdeveloped world.

ROBERT S. McNAMARA
President
International Bank for
Reconstruction and Development

CONTENTS

PREFACE   xi

I. INTRODUCTION   1

II. CHARACTERISTICS OF THE INDUSTRY   5
   Definition of Heavy Electrical Equipment   5
   The Products   6
   The Market   8
   Raw Materials and Semi-finished Components   8
   Technology   10
   Finance   11

III. THE INDUSTRY IN THE WORLD CONTEXT   12
   Production and Trade   12
   Dominance by Large International Concerns   14
   Capacity, Orders, Deliveries   17
   Mergers   21
   International Manufacturing Arrangements   22

IV. THE INDUSTRY IN DEVELOPING COUNTRIES   26
   Growth of the Industry   26
   Country Experiences   27
   Capabilities   36

V. PRICES FOR HEAVY ELECTRICAL EQUIPMENT   40
   World Market Prices   40

Prices in Developing Countries   43
The Moving Target   50
Light Industry   54

VI. COSTS AND COMPETITIVENESS   55
Concepts and Methodology   55
Materials   58
Manpower   62
Charges Against Capital   64
Combined Impact of Cost Differences   66
Measures of Competitiveness   66
Foreign Exchange Savings   74
Review of Findings   77

VII. THE DYNAMICS OF COMPETITIVENESS   80
Market   80
Learning Process   84
Institutional Framework   86

VIII. SUMMARY AND CONCLUSIONS   88

ANNEXES
A. Exchange Rate Adjustment in Argentina   96
B. Productivity and the Learning Process—Some Illustrations   98

TABLES

1. Maximum Specifications of Units Manufactured or in Process of Manufacture in European Countries, 1951, 1958 and 1967   7
2. Consumption of Heavy Electrical Equipment in 1965   13
3. Distribution of Exports of Nine Major Exporters, 1964   14
4. Major Producers of Heavy Electrical Equipment, 1964   15
5. Orders and Deliveries, 1964-67   18
6. The Maximum Size of Equipment Being Built by Domestic Manufacturers, 1967   37
7. Price Premia for Electrical Equipment in Developing Countries Compared with World Market Prices, 1964   46
8. Prices of Principal Materials, 1966   60
9. Comparison of Wages and Salaries, including All Supplementary Benefits, 1965   62

10. Employment and Manpower Cost against Sales, Heavy
    Electrical Equipment Industry, Seven Countries   64
11. Cost Structure in the Manufacture of Heavy Electrical
    Equipment   65
12. Measurement of Competitiveness—Example 1   68
13. Measurement of Competitiveness—Example 2   70
14. Measurement of Competitiveness—Example 3   72
15. Protection and Domestic Resource Cost per Unit of
    Foreign Exchange Saved for Twelve Individual Products   75
16. Measuring the Foreign Exchange Savings of the Industry,
    Six Countries, 1964   78

FIGURES

1. Evolution of Size of Vertical Generators, Spain, 1952–66   38
2. Development of Price Level for Hydroelectric Generators
    1956–65   44
3. Mexican Transformer Prices Compared with the Lowest
    International Bid, 1957–64   47
4. United States: Price Indices for Selected Products   50
5. United States: Average Transformer Prices by Size Groups,
    1958 and 1963   51
6. Price Indices of Distribution Transformers in Selected
    Countries   52
7. Price Indices of Rotating Machines in Selected Countries   52
8. Price of Distribution Transformers, Pakistan, Mexico,
    USA, 1965–66   53
9. Per Capita Spending on Heavy Electrical Equipment in
    Relation to GNP per Capita, 1964   81

ANNEX TABLES

1. Heavy Electrical Equipment Manufacturers: Structure of
    Assets and Liabilities, 1964   103
2. Export and Import of Heavy Electrical Equipment, 1965   104
3. Degrees of Self-Sufficiency in the Production of Electric
    Power Machinery and Switchgear, 1965   106
4. Maximum Specifications of Units Manufactured or in the
    Process of Manufacture, by Countries, January 1, 1967   107
5. Importance of Different Materials in Cost Structure for Power
    Transformers and Heavy Motors, Mexico, 1966   108
6. Cost Structure of a Generator, Argentina, 1965   109

7. Breakdown of Material Costs, Firms in Developing Countries, 1965 110
8. Inputs as percent of Total Material Cost, a Mexican Firm, 1964 and 1965 and a Pakistani Firm, 1965–66 111
9. Comparison of Direct Labor Requirements of Electrical Equipment, 1966 112
10. Manpower Costs in the Manufacture of Heavy Electrical Equipment, Related to Sales and Value Added, Industrial and Developing Countries, 1964 113
11. Price Assumptions for the Analysis in Chapter VI 114
12. Examples of the Calculation of Price Levels 114
13. Composition of Gross Profits, Profit-to-Sales and Sales to Assets Ratios for Representative European Manufacturers of Heavy Electrical Equipment 115
14. Production of Transformers by Manufacturers, India, 1962 116
15. Price Comparison of Transformers in Mexico 118
16. Price Indices for Mexican Large Motors Compared to Imports, 1966 120
17. International Bids—Comparison between Mexican Price and Lowest Foreign Price *c.i.f.* of Transformers, Mexico, 1957–64 121
18. Comparison of Prices of Motors in Mexico, India and Pakistan, 1965–66. 122

PREFACE

The study on the heavy electrical equipment industry is one of three case studies prepared as part of a broader research project dealing with the experience of the developing countries with the establishment of capital goods industries, which was under the direction of Barend A. de Vries. The case studies of industries, dealing with the automotive, heavy electrical and mechanical equipment industries, were directed by Bertil Walstedt. Herman van der Tak reviewed the studies in their later phase.

The industries selected for case studies play a strategic role in the more advanced phases of industrial development. Their establishment takes up a substantial share of investment and is, therefore, often accompanied by strains on real and financial resources and poses difficult problems of domestic and external economic policies. In addition, these industries produce many items used in the construction of the kind of projects financed by the Bank.

The industry studies were designed to consider the following questions:

— What has been the experience thus far of the industry in countries with relatively small markets?

— What are the economics of the industry in more advanced industrial countries and what are the conditions of international markets for the products concerned? What aspects are relevant for the growth of the industries in the developing countries?

— What are the costs and benefits of establishing these industries in developing countries? In particular, what is the cost of the saving of foreign exchange made possible by the industry?

— What can be said about the efficiency of the industry, at present and over time, and how is cost efficiency affected by such industrial factors as economies of scale, availability of supplier capabilities, skilled manpower, product design, access to new technology?

— What has been the impact upon the industry's cost efficiency of government policies—protection, exchange and import regulation, requirements as to domestic content of production, credit, etc.—as well as of the structure and the extent of monopoly of domestic industry?

— What general indications, if any, can be given on policies of developing countries, as well as of industrialized countries, to foster the healthy growth of the industry?

— What contributions might reasonably be expected from large multinational firms in promoting manufacturing in developing countries?

— What is the future outlook for the industries in an international context and what might be the manufacturing role of developing countries?

Because of the nature of the problems to be analyzed, heavy reliance had to be placed on direct interviews with, and information provided by, manufacturing concerns in developing countries and associated or parent firms in advanced industrial countries. The case studies are, therefore, largely based on findings from field visits to a number of developing countries which have experience with the capital goods industries, including Argentina, Brazil, India, Mexico, Pakistan and Spain. In addition, visits were made to firms in Europe and the United States.

Though the field visits were limited only to the developing countries indicated, and varied somewhat in their industry coverage, the interviews with multinational companies covered their operations in much of the developing world.

We are grateful to the various company representatives for their generous and invaluable assistance. They have shown great interest in the studies, have discussed the problems of the industry with frankness and made available information without which the study could not have been undertaken. They have supplied comments and criticisms on an earlier draft, permitting us to test the validity of the analysis and the accuracy of the factual information used.

The present study was undertaken by Mr. Ayhan Çilingiroḡlu aided by Mr. Jose Datas-Panero and Mr. Sanjaya Lall. Miss Helen May and Miss Ediana

Harahap contributed much of the statistical work. There were also helpful criticisms and suggestions by electrical equipment manufacturers and by other experts both inside and outside the World Bank Group. The author alone, of course, is responsible for the facts and opinions presented. The views expressed in this paper are in no way to be taken as necessarily representing the views of the World Bank.

ANDREW M. KAMARCK
Director
Economics Department

I

INTRODUCTION

This study analyzes factors in the growth and competitiveness of the heavy electrical equipment industry in developing countries. For the purpose of the study the heavy electrical equipment industry is defined as the *manufacture* of equipment for power generation, transmission, and sometimes industry (e.g. large motors and electric furnaces). It does not cover communication equipment and consumer durables (automotive parts or domestic appliances) of any kind. Electric locomotives and cables are also excluded.

The study is based on findings from field trips to Argentina, Brazil, Mexico, Pakistan and Spain, on documentation available in the World Bank on the Indian industry, and on interviews with sixteen major international manufacturers in the United States and Western Europe. The field trips were limited to developing countries with advanced development in electrical equipment manufacturing, but an attempt was made to cover the rest of the developing world by means of interviews with international companies. The main focus of the study is on the comparison of prices and costs in developing countries with those in the international market. The three chapters following this one review the distinguishing characteristics of the industry while the three chapters thereafter discuss factors affecting its competitiveness—international prices, factor costs and production efficiency in the developing countries, and factors which may affect comparative costs over time. The final chapter summarizes the study and indicates main findings.

1

While Chapter II deals with some of the general features of the industry, Chapter III describes the international structure of its production and trade. Because of heavy concentration in the international market (about 20 firms cover 90 percent of the world trade) and the fact that all manufacturers in developing countries are linked with international manufacturers—either through capital participation or licensing agreements or both—a knowledge of the international structure is essential for understanding the problems which face the developing world.

Reviews of some individual country experiences are given in Chapter IV to provide a comparative picture of the industry. The historical background and current status of the industry are briefly discussed in terms of physical capacities, technical capabilities and major problems.

Any international comparison of values is affected by the rates of exchange (or rates of conversion) used. There is an obvious difficulty in arriving at a reasonable cost figure for production of a heavy electrical product with a long lead time (over a year or more) during periods of rapid inflation. Moreover, successive devaluations make international comparisons extremely complicated. For instance, in Brazil there were three devaluations within two years (1964–1965); thus the costs of producing a generator over several months cannot simply be added up in cruzeiros. In the majority of countries studied, over-valuation of the currency has been compensated by high tariffs. Quantitative restrictions, and sometimes prohibition of particular imports, introduce other dimensions in determining the domestic prices of imported goods. Complex exchange systems, e.g. multiple exchange rates, compulsory deposits, and surcharges, are among the elements which cause difficulties. The problem is particularly difficult in Argentina and Brazil, and we have derived exchange rates for these two countries. (See Annex A.) The basic Indian data for this study was collected before devaluation. Thus the old rupee rate (Rs. 4.75 = US $1) has been used.

Quality is another issue to be considered when comparing costs and prices for products as well as inputs. Since manufacturers in developing countries are linked with international manufacturers, the products they offer under international competition are generally based on the latest designs. Despite this there are great differences in production technology and in quality between products with a high domestic content and those sold in the international market. Efforts to maximize domestic content impose a strain both on manufacturing facilities and on the product. Their impact on operational difficulties in developing countries (additional maintenance requirements, frequencies of shut-downs, etc.) can only be evaluated after several years. The industry is young in most developing countries; therefore quality differences have been described rather than measured.

Chapter V reviews world market prices in some detail and compares them with prices in developing countries. All information on prices is based on actual transactions. It is important to bear in mind that the prices of heavy electrical equipment are irregular and are not like prices of items such as steel, cement, or fertilizers for which continuous price information is quoted in trade journals. Any price comparison is true only for *the product* at *the time* of purchase in *the country* under *the set of conditions* (financial arrangements, political motivations, etc.) prevailing. Deriving a price pattern or reference level, as we attempt to do in this study, requires a very large sample because of the custom-derived nature of product and prices alike.

Because of the scattered price information and the great variety of products, the price comparisons in Chapter V are incomplete. The cost comparisons of major raw materials in Chapter VI are more complete because, in contrast to the prices of final products, the prices of material inputs are relatively easy to obtain. About 90 percent of the total material cost is composed of six or eight materials (copper, silicon steel sheets, ordinary steel, paper, porcelain, ferrous and nonferrous castings). The basic material mix for a given product may vary under different manufacturing conditions. First, there may be a difference in quality of raw materials (e.g. non-uniform thickness of steel sheets); secondly, the working scrap ratio in a less advanced manufacturing environment is higher; and thirdly, larger pieces of material of higher grade may be used for less demanding jobs because the right ones are not immediately available—for instance, thick carbon steel plates may be used for transformer tanks where thinner plates would do.

Chapters VI and VII analyze the conditions for economic production in terms of four major determinants—the sum of factor costs (materials, labor, capital), the size of the market, the learning process, and finally, what, for want of a better word, is termed the "institutional framework" (mainly government policies). In a sense, the first three factors represent a country's intrinsic comparative advantage. The fourth factor determines whether a latent potential can be translated into actual competitiveness. The results of the evaluation of actual costs and foreign exchange savings in Chapter VI should be looked upon not as an indication of the differing success of developing countries, but as a comparison of a developing country's industry with the international market at a particular time. Some dynamic factors are considered in Chapter VII. Chapter VIII provides a summary of the study and its findings.

In this study we distinguish factors inherent in the industry (type and nature of product, cost structure), from factors controlled to some extent by corporate management (cost, price), and from other factors not so controlled (size of market, institutional framework, etc.). We have not made specific policy recommendations for the parties concerned—manufacturers, developing coun-

3

tries, development agencies. In general, the study leads to the conclusion that corporations would profit by learning to look upon the world not only as one market but also as one manufacturing base; developing countries would benefit by following carefully what happens in the international market; and, consequently, development agencies should encourage such efforts.

II

CHARACTERISTICS OF THE INDUSTRY

Definition of Heavy Electrical Equipment

In our study the term "heavy electrical equipment" includes equipment for the generation and transmission of electric power and for certain major industrial uses. The principal products are main line generators, power transformers, switchgear, rectifiers, large motors and electric furnaces. Light motors and distribution transformers have been excluded, as have wire and cable. Though some electrical equipment manufacturers make wire and cable, much output also comes from specialized producers in the nonferrous metals and rubber industries. On the other hand, steam turbines have been included in some of our trade and production figures. Though by technology an item of mechanical equipment, steam turbines have traditionally been supplied by electrical equipment manufacturers as a major component in complete steam power generating plants. Nevertheless, since steam turbines are not generally produced in developing countries,[1] no comparative analysis has been made for this line.

Heavy equipment is normally made to individual design. It requires considerable investment in special testing facilities and in heavy handling and machinery facilities. The production cycle is long, varying from 18 to 24 months for very large equipment, and from 8 to 12 months for smaller ones. The concept of *heavy*, as just defined, forms the basis for specialization by some

---

[1] With exceptions such as India and Spain.

5

major firms and, more commonly, for the separation of heavy equipment divisions from others within large international concerns. These divisions, of course, may not coincide exactly with our definition. Thus, small generators, transformers, and switchgear may be produced separately from the larger units. Where the market is large, smaller units may be produced in series, and different manufacturing techniques may be adopted.

Within the heavy equipment category, there is a significant difference between equipment at the heavy end of the range and equipment at the light end. To avoid confusion the terms "large" and "small" will be used to indicate such differences in size, or the range of power or voltage will be given. In developing countries with low domestic and industrial consumption, individual generators and transformers are likely to be relatively small. Again, since individual regions are often unconnected with one another or with large power sources, at least in the early stages, transmission lines usually have low voltages. In this respect, there could theoretically be a certain harmony between the development of the power network and the development of the technical capability of the local industry. An industry could gain experience on equipment of medium sizes before tackling very heavy and complex ones.

Our study is focused on the conditions for developing countries to enter the manufacture of heavy electrical equipment on an economic basis. It includes therefore countries which have taken only partial steps in that direction (Mexico), or may be on the verge of entry (Pakistan), as well as those which are more advanced (e.g. Spain and Brazil). This has led us, in some cases, to investigate how well countries such as Mexico and Pakistan are doing with products representative of their present level of technical capability; these products may, at least in part, fall below the range we have defined as "heavy equipment." This has led us to distinguish three categories of electrical equipment—large, intermediate and small. They are rough divisions, and their border lines may vary according to the country, the age of the industry and other factors.

The Products

Though there is a tendency to apply mass production methods to the manufacture of distribution transformers and small-size steam turbines, the main characteristic of the industry is the custom-designed nature of its products, which are in general very large units. This calls for ability to design according to the customer's specification, and for highly skilled workmanship at the bench level to interpret drawings and to carry the responsibility for independent jobs on large pieces with very small tolerances. Manufacturing techniques vary greatly with the type and size of product.

6

Economies of scale in power generation and transmission (or sometimes the geographical remoteness of major power sources) have forced the industry to strive for higher voltages and to concentrate enormous power in single units, i.e. on a single axis (Table 1). Before the 1950's the maximum commercial A.C. transmission voltage was 220 kv; in the last decade this has been raised to 400–500 kv. At present the effort is to obtain 750 kv or more. Similarly, not more than ten years ago the largest turbine built in Europe was at the most 200 MW, whereas in 1966 the European firms were manufacturing sizes about 600 MW and the capacities now are around 1000 MW. *Higher* voltages place new strains upon the supplier industries (especially for insulation material), necessitate special techniques and equipment for manufacture and testing, and also take up more space. *Large* equipment also requires higher quality components (forgings and castings especially) and larger, more powerful production equipment and facilities.

TABLE 1: **Maximum Specifications of Units Manufactured or in Process of Manufacture in European Countries, 1951, 1958 and 1967**

	Unit	1951	1958	1967
Steam turbines				
Rating	MW	110	250	660
Maximum pressure	kg/cm^2	89	145	250
Maximum temperature	°C	520	565	565
Thermal generators	MW	125	300	660
Hydraulic generators	MW	160	180	242
Transformers	Mva	200[a]	900[b]	1,000

[a] Three separate phases.
[b] Three of 300 Mva single phase units.
Source: Organization for Economic Cooperation and Development, *Twentieth Survey of Electric Power Equipment* (Paris, 1967).

The size of the equipment ordered today is so large and construction periods are so long that at a given moment one unit or one order may be taking up 20–25 percent of the production capacity of a plant. The unit may be on the factory floor for a year—generally even longer. The programming of overall production is rendered extremely difficult by the irregularity of orders and the size of each individual order. Large orders and long lead times demand large amounts of working capital. The need for fixed capital has increased because economies of scale in selling costs and in research and development, as well as the marketing advantages of offering a full line of equipment, have prompted most of the international firms to manufacture practically every type of heavy electrical equipment.

7

Manufacturing techniques vary with the product group. The manufacture of transformers, which are static equipment, differs from making switchgear and rotating machines, and among rotating machines, steam equipment is very different from a hydroelectric generator. In the largest international concerns, plants are often specialized in a given type of equipment. This variety of heavy electrical equipment adds another difficulty for developing countries.

The Market

The customers for heavy electrical equipment are generally large concerns: power companies, railroads, and large industrial firms. The number of customers is limited, sometimes to a single customer. Thus, in France, Electricité de France accounts for something like 40 percent of the market, the French State Railways (SNCF) for another 30 percent.

Electrical equipment is always subject to regulations and minimum specifications for safety. Also, each customer has certain standards and rules of his own, and evaluates each tender on the basis of a "rationale" developed over the years. Customer preferences are based not only on price and quality but also on the suitability of the equipment for the existing system, the experience gained by manufacturers on similar work and the relation between manufacturers and purchasers. The price of heavy electrical equipment, in fact, is part of a package which includes many non-price elements such as speed of delivery, credit terms, ease of ordering, and quality of after-sale services. These non-price factors explain some of the preference enjoyed by local manufacturers in their national markets.

If manufacturers are tied essentially to a local market, the regularity of ordering by the main local purchasers becomes highly significant. A manufacturer of heavy electrical equipment has a high investment in fixed assets and in a highly specialized staff and labor force. Unless he can ensure reasonably stable utilization for these resources, operations will be neither profitable nor economical.

Raw Materials and Semi-finished Components

Material costs dominate factory costs; they are 77 percent of ex-factory cost for a transformer in Mexico, for instance (see Annex Table 5). The most important raw materials for the heavy electrical equipment industry are copper wire or bars and silicon steel sheets. For example, in a transformer manufactured in Brazil, copper accounts for 23 percent and silicon steel for 40 percent of total material costs. Ordinary steel sheets are also important, as are bearings and insulation materials such as paper, porcelain bushings and transformer oil. These materials are imported by most countries and are normally freely available on the world market at established prices. Though supply difficulties in copper in 1964–65 led to a disorganized price structure, it is difficult to identify any important long-run cost advantages for any country or firm with respect to supplies of primary copper. Nor is there much advantage in firms manufacturing their own silicon sheets. On the other hand, a competitive disadvantage may arise for some developing countries where protection has raised prices for semi-manufactures of copper, aluminum, or the like.

Steel castings and forgings as well as nonferrous castings are used quite extensively by the manufacturers of heavy electrical equipment, as well as by other branches of engineering industries. In industrialized countries there are specialized foundries and forging plants from which heavy electrical equipment manufacturers purchase their requirements of semi-finished parts while the manufacturers themselves concentrate on design, machining, electrical engineering and assembly. In developing countries, however, the heavy electrical equipment industry is often forced to establish its own facilities for casting, forging and the like. Electrical equipment manufacturers in Pakistan are even forced to make their own nuts and bolts. Even where outside suppliers are used, electrical equipment manufacturers must often help them with financing and technical assistance.

The establishment by electrical equipment manufacturers of special facilities for the production of parts, coupled with the protection offered to local suppliers of cable, wire, bushings, etc., has raised production costs in several of the countries studied. Though electrical equipment manufacturers are large buyers, they have had to accept high costs (even where these are caused by monopolistic pricing practices) as a price paid for the desire of the local government to industrialize and to save foreign exchange. There has been resistance (not always successful) when the quality of the local product is inferior; power companies, for obvious reasons, are concerned about the performance of their equipment.

Heavy electrical equipment, simply because of its size and nature, offers substantial savings in freight and handling when partly built or assembled in the country. Some international firms have developed special designs suitable to local manufacturing capabilities, e.g. parts normally produced by cast steel are replaced by welded pieces, etc. Thus, a German company developed a design for the Estreito Power Plant in Brazil by which they obtained a 60 percent reduction of the weight to be shipped, and arrived at a 33 percent domestic contribution (= savings in foreign exchange based upon *c.i.f.* value).

9

Though the basic principles in the construction of heavy electrical equipment have remained the same since the beginning of the industry, there has been a steady stream of technological improvements and some major breakthroughs. Patented inventions now cover almost every component and manufacturing process. These have been directed, in part, towards the reduction of electrical losses and also towards the manufacture of lighter and more compact equipment.[2] But, from the beginning, the main thrust of technological progress has been in the capability of designing and producing the ever larger equipment demanded by customers. In this respect the industry may now be close to a ceiling since the enormous size of some modern equipment causes many difficulties in transport, handling and operation. On the other hand, this situation also presents a challenge to introduce revolutionary changes in the generation, transmission and application of power.

The introduction of nuclear energy for power generation has been a major revolution for the power supply industry, and has had important repercussions on the electrical equipment industry. All major electrical equipment manufacturers have become involved not only in the construction of steam power plants based upon nuclear energy (generally very large plants calling for new design and technology), but also in the construction of nuclear reactors, an entirely new line of activity. This has necessitated tremendous research expenditure. It has brought substantial business and prospective large earnings, a new future and perspective to some firms (e.g. General Electric, USA), while some other firms have had bitter experiences, and their overall results have been badly affected. For equipment manufacturers in developing countries, the long-run implications of the change towards nuclear power are probably on balance unfavorable. On the one hand, phasing out of hydropower production in many industrialized countries would rob these countries of advantages previously enjoyed by virtue of a large home market and continual improvements in technology. A country like Brazil could then emerge as an exporter of the hydroelectric generators and turbines which will still be demanded. On the other hand, none of the developing countries have proceeded very far in the production of steam power generating equipment. Entry into this field, which is based upon the supply of large-scale nuclear power stations, will be much more difficult and costly than it would have been in the past, when it was based upon moderate-sized conventional steam power stations.

---

[2] For instance, the introduction of cooled conductors has brought about reduction in weight and also improvement in efficiency in production leading to a cost reduction and finally to a cut in prices.

Finance

Availability of finance, judging from statements made to our research team, appears to be a very important condition for successful operation in the manufacture of heavy electrical equipment. This is particularly true for export sales and for sales of heavy electrical equipment in developing countries.

This financing problem does not arise from a high ratio of fixed assets to sales; in this respect, the manufacture of heavy electrical equipment would not seem to be a particularly capital-intensive industry. Rather it arises from the need to tie up substantial funds in work-in-process and in receivables.[3] The impact of such heavy working capital requirements is aggravated by typically longer production periods in developing countries. In many of the countries studied, there have also been delays in payments for work done and difficulties in the orderly scheduling of materials, whether imported or local. Finally, in inflationary economies like Brazil and Argentina, grave problems are posed for financial management, purchasing policies, and forward pricing. In part, these problems are the foreseeable costs of working in a developing economy. In part, however, they reflect avoidable institutional shortcomings.

We have focused, above, on finance as it affects the supplier of electrical equipment. Finance in the form of equipment credit is also important in the buyer's choice. Many power companies in developing countries are short of funds for expansion. Yet delay in construction may be more costly both to the power companies and to the economy than even a sizeable difference in the original cost. Exporters in industrial countries are well supported, both by their governments and their banking connections, in granting long-term credits; similar assistance to manufacturers in developing countries is essential if they are to compete on reasonably equal terms with imports.

In the case of partial production in developing countries, financing of the domestic contribution may present a problem because of a lack of institutions interested in financing such operations. Export financing institutions of industrial countries are reluctant to finance local costs in the importing countries. This often puts an additional burden on the international company otherwise willing to procure a large part of the order locally.

---

[3] Some illustrative figures regarding the composition of assets and of assets-to-sales ratios are shown in Annex Table 1.

III

THE INDUSTRY IN THE WORLD CONTEXT

Production and Trade

The total annual world demand for heavy electrical equipment (including steam turbines and related equipment) is about US $16 billion, of which 80 percent comes from ten industrialized countries. Another ten countries, as shown in Table 2, account for a further 7 percent. The largest market by far is the United States with annual purchases of $8 billion; it accounts for nearly one half of total world demand. Next are Germany, the United Kingdom and France. Among the developing countries the largest markets are Spain, India, Mexico, Brazil and Argentina; the experience of these countries plus Pakistan will be reviewed in Chapter IV.

Trade in heavy electrical equipment for a substantial number of countries is given in Annex Table 2. The five countries with the largest markets (USA, Germany, UK, France and Japan) are also net exporters of electrical equipment. Because of specialization, however, all these countries except the United States import part of their domestic requirements (between 8 and 15 percent). Annex Table 2 shows that Austria, Italy and Switzerland are also net exporters, although these countries rely more heavily on imports, which represent from 20 to 45 percent of domestic consumption. Belgium, the Netherlands, and Sweden are net importers of equipment to differing degrees of dependence. Canada is also a net importer of machinery. Although its exports

TABLE 2: Consumption of Heavy Electrical Equipment in 1965[a]

(US $ million)

USA	8,000	Netherlands	154
Germany	1,064	Switzerland	150
UK	950	Spain	140
France	822	India	133
Japan	522	Mexico	126
Canada	481	Denmark	96
Italy	443	Brazil	94
Australia	231	Austria	93
Sweden	191	South Africa	77
Belgium	154	Argentina	75
Total, countries shown			13,000
Estimated world total[a]			16,000

[a] Excludes the USSR, other Eastern bloc countries, and Mainland China. Includes all categories shown in Annex Table 2, though that table also includes some light equipment. If we exclude steam turbines and related equipment, the demand would be about US $10 or $11 billion.

Source: Rough approximations supplied by the courtesy of an international manufacturer.

are small, Canada's imports represent only about 27 percent of total consumption. The other countries shown in the table are substantial net importers. Their imports ranged in 1965 from 26 percent of total consumption in Brazil to nearly the entire consumption in India.

There are in fact two strategies for the development of a viable heavy electrical industry. Annex Table 3 shows that one group of heavy electrical producers (USA, Germany, UK, France) import relatively little of their consumption. (See the last column of that table.) Another group (the Netherlands, Italy, Austria especially) import more freely but export over half their annual production; they pursue an open market policy with success.

The importance of trade, even among industrialized countries, indicates the advantages of specialization where technical progress is rapid and world market prices low. Most major manufacturing countries build thermal electric generators of up to 200 MW, hydropower generators of up to 100 MW and transformers of up to 300 Mva. But beyond these limits different countries have pushed their capabilities in different directions.[1] Even the United States is not in the technological forefront of all types, and not always competitive in terms of price.

Total world exports of heavy electrical equipment (including Eastern Bloc countries) amount to $2.5 billion annually, of which nearly 60 percent go to

---

[1] See Annex Table 4 for production capabilities, by countries, in major lines of equipment (1967).

industrial countries and the remainder to developing countries. Total exports in 1964 and their direction for the nine major exporting countries are given in Table 3.

TABLE 3: Distribution of Exports of Nine Major Exporters, 1964

	Exports (US $ million) to:			Country's % Share in Exports to:	
Exporting Country	All countries	Industrial countries	Developing countries	Industrial countries	Developing countries
USA	670	314	356	36	31
Germany	470	118	352	13	31
UK	270	127	143	15	12
France	181	98	83	11	7
Japan	137	33	104	4	9
Switzerland	101	73	28	8	3
Italy	95	34	61	4	5
Sweden	70	56	14	6	1
Canada	34	22	12	3	1
	2,028	875	1,153	100	100

Sources: Trade statistics of individual countries.

The distribution of exports forms an interesting pattern, which has evolved according to such factors as political links, tied aid, and the shift to new sources of procurement such as Japan instead of the USA in South East Asia and Europe instead of the USA in Latin America. It can be seen that Germany, Japan and Italy sold most of their exports to developing countries, while Sweden, Canada and Switzerland sold mostly to industrialized countries. The developing countries import, in particular, hydraulic generating equipment, transformers and switchgear. About 55 percent of all transformer exports and 64 percent of all switchgear exports went to these areas. Industrial countries imported mainly thermal generating, industrial, and traction equipment.

Dominance by Large International Concerns

The heavy electrical equipment industry is controlled by a few international firms of large size, many of which have very diversified production lines including all types and sizes of electrical equipment, domestic appliances, communication equipment, and electronic equipment. Table 4 below shows the major producers in different countries and their total sales and employment (including products other than heavy electrical equipment). The largest pro-

TABLE 4: Major Producers of Heavy Electrical Equipment, 1964

	Employment	Total Sales (US $ million)
USA		
General Electric	300,000	4,941.4
Westinghouse	114,000	2,271.2
UK		
Associated Electric Industries[g]	91,000	662.5
English Electric (1965)[g]	70,000	686.0
GEC (1962)[g]	38,000[a]	379.0
C. A. Parsons	12,000[b]	n.a.
A. Reyrolle & Co.	9,000	n.a.
Germany		
Siemens-Schuckertwerke (1965)[c]	84,900	700.0
AEG[d]	67,700	610.0
Brown Boveri Co. (Germany)	38,000	264.0
France		
CGE	52,000	678.0
Alsthom	15,000	155.0
CEM (1965)	11,000	121.0
Japan		
Hitachi	123,900	1,010.0
Tokyo Shibaura Electric Co. (Toshiba)	112,000	860.0
Mitsubishi Electric Corporation	57,000	560.0
Switzerland		
Brown Boveri Co. (Switzerland)[e]	16,000[b]	132.0
Oerlikon (1965)	4,500[b]	40.0
Sweden		
ASEA[f]	33,398	400.0
Belgium		
ACEC	15,600[b]	127.0
Italy[a]		
Ercole Marelli	n.a.	110.0
CGE	n.a.	46.4
Ansaldo S. Giorgio	n.a.	28.2
Tecnomasio Italiano Brown Boveri S.A.	–	28.0
Austria		
Elin	8,500[b]	60.7

[a] 1965.

[b] 1966.

[c] This refers to the position in 1965; since then Siemens Halske A.G. (electronics and telecommunication), Siemens-Schuckertwerke A.G. and Siemens-Reinigerwerke A.G. (medical and laboratory equipment) have combined to become Siemens A.G. In 1967 the whole Siemens group employed 240,000; AEG Telefunken, 135,000.

[d] Excluding Telefunken.

[e] For the whole Brown Boveri Group (at present 18 manufacturing companies) total employment would be 76,000 and total sales $740 million in 1967.

[f] The ASEA group as a whole.

[g] GEC merged with AEI in 1967 and with English Electric in 1969. Reyrolle and Parsons have also merged.

Source: Figures are based upon 1964 Annual Reports unless otherwise stated.

ducers of heavy electrical equipment are General Electric and Westinghouse, followed by GEC—English Electric and Siemens. The firms most specialized within the industry are Parsons (large rotating machines), Alsthom and CEM (generation and traction equipment), Brown Boveri, Elin, ASEA and ACEC.

The large international firms predominate in the production of generators, turbines and switchgear. Certain items like very large steam turbines and generators or high-voltage D.C. transmission equipment are even the exclusive domain of a few firms. Even in transformers, which are the most common product of the industry, the large firms take the lion's share. In the world, there are about 250 manufacturers of power and distribution transformers, employing altogether about 120,000 people—of these, about 25 firms employ 90,000 (75 percent of the labor force) and account for all the exports.

In the light of the prevalence of across-the-board capital participations and know-how agreements, there is substantial scope for coordinated action by the major producers. General Electric of the United States and Brown Boveri of Switzerland are probably the two companies with the largest capital participations in other major producing countries. Besides its considerable equity interests in Spanish and Italian firms, GE owns about 10 percent of the equity of AEG of Germany and has been active in restoring its prewar position in France. Brown Boveri, Switzerland, owns Brown Boveri, Mannheim (the third largest manufacturer in Germany), Tecnomasio Italiano Brown Boveri of Italy, and is also the largest shareholder of CEM of France. France's Jeumont-Schneider (itself a recent merger between Jeumont and Schneider-Westinghouse) is controlled by the Empain group which owns ACEC of Belgium. Westinghouse is now interested in taking over the Empain interests to form a European grouping which it will dominate.

Concentration of control is even more pronounced with respect to know-how than with respect to manufacturing operations. General Electric has know-how exchange agreements with AEG (Germany), Alsthom (France), AEI (United Kingdom), and Toshiba (Japan), ASGEN (Italy), etc. Westinghouse has agreements with Siemens (Germany), Jeumont-Schneider (France), ACEC (Belgium), English Electric (UK), Marelli (Italy), Mitsubishi (Japan).

This concentration of know-how is expected to increase in the future because of the limited resources allocated to research and development by European firms as compared with American firms. The total research budget of Westinghouse is more than twice the total business of some very sizeable European firms, and it is generally believed that the research carried out by General Electric has been an important factor in explaining the profitability of that corporation. On the other hand, judging only from the past, giant

16

size and a large research budget may not be indispensable conditions for success, as shown by the business results of companies like ASEA (Sweden) and Brown Boveri (Switzerland).

Capacity, Orders, Deliveries

The existence of large unused capacity is not new to the heavy electrical industry. Some observers have related it to cartel-type price arrangements, and to procurement policies by national power companies, which have permitted an excessive number of firms to share in existing business rather than to compete, rationalize, and reorganize. However this may be, the problem has been accentuated in recent years by the increased size of individual generators and transformers. The creation of the Common Market and the European Free Trade Area have brought attention to the excessive number of producers in the industry. In the United States there are only two producers of steam turbines (Allis-Chalmers having withdrawn from the field) sharing a market of more than 30 million kw per year. Though the market in the whole of Western Europe is only about eight million kw per year, there are 11 manufacturers in the Common Market alone. The situation is not much different in hydro-electric generators.

The growing sizes of power equipment, which has led to a decrease in the number of units to be produced, has left only very few large generating units to be delivered within a year by the entire industry (three units of 500 MW within three years by all French industry). If there are many manufacturers the number of units to be purchased by power companies would not be sufficient to give a sizeable order to each company. This has led power companies to exercise pressure on their domestic industries to combine manufacturing facilities, and thereby also to become technologically more competitive in international markets. For instance Electricité de France undoubtedly feels some responsibility for the advancement of the French electrical industry in the European Common Market context.

Power networks have become more integrated and now are able technically to accommodate much larger equipment. Since most power networks are very large and are connected internationally, failure of one unit such as a 600 MW would not disturb the power supply greatly. The use of large units brings substantial savings in the total cost of power plants. Economies of scale in the power industry are such that the cost of one 600 MW turbine-generator set is only 1.5 times (not twice) the price of one 300 MW unit. Besides this price difference, there are enormous savings in transport, construction and maintenance costs.

Table 5 shows the steady growth of deliveries in all sectors of production

17

TABLE 5: Orders and Deliveries, 1964–67

		Deliveries	New Orders	Orders in hand[e] January 1	Orders in hand /Deliveries
		(1)	(2)	(3)	(3) ÷ (1)
Europe					
Generators for steam turbines (MW)[a]	1964	14,665	20,535		
	1965	16,521	19,338	59,170	3.58
	1966	19,507	14,242	61,987	3.18
	1967[d]	23,648		56,722	2.40
Generators for water turbines (MW)[a]	1964	5,531	3,947		
	1965	4,917	8,284	13,775	2.80
	1966	6,269	3,216	17,142	2.73
	1967[d]	7,936		14,089	1.78
Power transformers (Mva)[b]	1964	105,095	105,938		
	1965	99,996	100,330	223,563	2.24
	1966	103,307	92,246	217,982	2.11
	1967[d]	119,905		206,921	1.73
Nuclear power reactors (MWe)	1965	2,015	750		
	1966	1,312	2,156	4,527	3.45
	1967	1,293		5,396	4.17
USA					
Generators for steam turbines (MW)[a]	1964	12,394	21,112		
	1965	13,744	26,975	42,496	3.09
	1966	15,492	47,023	55,444	3.58
	1967[d]	24,364		87,159	3.58
Generators for water turbines (MW)[c]	1964	2,397	5,477		
	1965	1,621	2,504	9,347	5.77
	1966	3,071	1,002	10,230	3.33
	1967[d]	3,414		8,161	2.39
Power transformers (Mva)[b]	1964	68,967	100,613		
	1965	80,248	107,838	121,066	1.51
	1966	102,146	153,103	145,864	1.43
	1967[d]	116,031		190,825	1.64
Nuclear power reactors (MWe)	1966	926	..	..	
	1967	2,420	..	26,441	10.9
Japan					
Generators for steam turbines (MW)[a]	1964	2,318	2,137		
	1965	2,954	3,457	4,510	1.53
	1966	2,930	3,688	4,714	1.61
	1967[d]	2,812		5,765	2.05
Generators for water turbines (MW)[a]	1964	1,755	749		
	1965	1,078	2,460	1,365	1.27
	1966	827	3,883	3,222	3.90
	1967[d]	2,119		6,351	3.00
Power transformers (Mva)[b]	1964	17,452	24,471		
	1965	22,268	26,895	24,189	1.09
	1966	20,792	22,800	28,969	1.39
	1967[d]	25,497		29,124	1.14

Table notes on p. 19.

(except nuclear power plant in Europe). It is otherwise with new orders. In Europe these have fallen over the years 1964–67 in all categories except nuclear power (and gas turbines). In the USA, on the other hand, the orders for nearly all equipment have been increasing, with one important exception; in hydro equipment, Japanese industry has been gaining orders while US industry has been losing them. For manufacturers everywhere, excess capacity, or the expectation of excess capacity in the future, is crucial in influencing their bidding policies. Hence the ratio of orders in hand to deliveries is significant. In Europe, this ratio has been falling steadily for all conventional plant.

The best hydroelectric resources of Europe, the USA and Japan are by now exhausted. And since 1960 the greater part of production of hydroelectric plant is for export. More important, conventional thermal as well as nuclear power generation and transmission is undergoing steady technical and economic improvement. Thus although worldwide demand is still rising, effects of excess capacity are likely to be experienced in two sectors now bypassed by modern trends: a) hydroelectric equipment and b) steam power equipment below the size now being demanded in industrial countries.

To produce a steam turbine of 50 megawatts capacity requires in Europe 60,000 man-hours, whereas a 100 megawatt unit requires only 80,000 man-hours. Production of one 100 MW unit requires the holding of more materials and stock at one time and demands more powerful manufacturing capacities (larger building, longer lathes, heavier cranes, higher assembly shops, etc.). The manufacture of such units, if never undertaken before, requires very large research and development expenditure. When purchasers buy two 600 MW turbines to meet a given power demand instead of buying six 200 MW units, there is work for only two firms, since production of steam turbines can hardly be broken down to small fractions, and purchasers like to have only one major equipment supplier for a project. Therefore less work is shared by the industry. Yet an individual firm's R & D expenditures and additional investments, etc. will be much higher. This favors the trend towards concentration.

---

[a] 10 MW units upwards.
[b] 10 Mva units upwards.
[c] 4 MW units upwards.
[d] Orders booked at January 1/67 for delivery in 1967. Japan: orders booked at April 1/67 for delivery in 1967.
[e] Japan: orders booked at April 1 of the year in question.
Note: New orders (+) and deliveries (−) do not entirely account for the differences in orders in hand between one year and the next. The balance is evidently explained by cancellations.
Source: Organization for Economic Cooperation and Development: *Nineteenth and Twentieth Surveys of Electric Power Equipment* (Paris, 1966 and 1967).

Another example can be given from the transformer market in the United Kingdom in 1967:

In consequence [*of ever larger transformer sizes*] the average price of transformers remained at about £1 [then US $2.80] per kva from 1930 to 1960 and has dropped slightly since then. With the smaller distribution transformers . . . prices now barely cover variable costs. With the big transformers . . . last year [1966] prices came down 20 percent. Even then manufacturers of the size of A.E.I., Bruce Peebles and C. A. Parsons got no new transformer orders from the Central Electricity Generating Board. This year manufacturers were bracing themselves for another round of cuts of up to 30 percent. At this point the C.E.G.B. saw trouble ahead. Once prices get below even variable costs a manufacturer can increase his profits by simply closing his factory. . . . Prices for this year's orders will be 'frozen', in the sense that the C.E.G.B. will not let them go down any further. It will be ordering at last year's prices. There is enough capacity in Britain to make about £46 million of grid transformers (200 kv and above) a year. In 1964, when the C.E.G.B.'s orders were over £35 million, the industry was only 80 percent loaded. Its break-even point is around 70 percent. But the current ordering rate is only around £18 million [i.e. *less than 40 percent capacity utilization*] . . . knocking the big eight manufacturers down to four would not be so difficult.[2]

Excess capacity, large capital requirements for research and development, high overhead costs, lumpy or fluctuating demand, and the fear of competition because of regional trade agreements, are the factors which explain the pressure on prices and the pressure for mergers and/or "arrangements" among producers. In competitive conditions this pressure also gives a strong incentive to producers to seek separate markets in order to minimize price competition. Thus, excess capacity also explains the jealous protection of national markets and the attempts to extend these protected markets abroad through various financial and other arrangements.

Finally, such pressures explain *both* the very sharp price competition on the free world market *and* attempts to get around this competition by licensing agreements with firms working in protected markets or direct investment in such firms. An international cartel known as I.N.C.A. (International Notification and Compensation Agreement) was in operation in the early 1930's.[3] In the late 1950's and early 1960's the producers in the USA made an agree-

---

[2] *The Economist*, May 20, 1967, pp. 820–823. There are now only two or three big manufacturers.

[3] See: *Report of the Federal Trade Commission on International Electrical Equipment Cartels*, U.S. Government Printing Office, 1948.

ment on price fixing, which was stopped by court action.[4] If attempts to reform an international cartel have been made subsequently, they do not appear to have been successful.[5]

Mergers

Leading manufacturers have tended to produce a full line of heavy electrical equipment. This has made them less vulnerable to fluctuations in the demand for individual items and has had certain advantages in competing for jobs for complete power plants and in relations with suppliers (because of the large total volume of orders). The speed of technological progress today is such, however, that enormous investments would be needed to keep in the forefront of technology over a wide front. In France, this problem has been partially solved by Electricité de France bearing a considerable portion of total research and development costs. Electricité de France has also become more courageous in its order policy, encouraging new techniques, e.g. for large units. In Germany, on the other hand, the several power companies provide little support to the research effort of the German heavy electrical equipment industry. Hence, in spite of the size of individual companies, this industry has lagged behind other countries, e.g. in steam turbines. It is only recently that German power companies have taken a step towards large units; they have ordered two nuclear reactors of 600 MW and related equipment.

The movement towards mergers has changed the structure of the industry, especially in Europe. The main manufacturers of heavy electrical equipment in the United Kingdom were AEI and English Electric, which were formed through mergers of several companies, and C. A. Parsons, which bought the business of General Electric Company (UK) in rotating machines, and has now joined with Reyrolle. In September 1967, Johnson and Phillips Ltd. were taken over by English Electric. Then GEC, more successful profit-wise than its rivals, bid first for AEI and then for English Electric, which merged with GEC in January 1969. In 1965, two major French producers, Alsthom and CGE, decided to merge some of their operations to form one new company, Delle-Alsthom, for the production of high and medium voltage switchgear, and another company, Alsthom-Savoisienne, for large transformers. CGE holds the majority of the shares in the first company while Alsthom is the leading shareholder in the second. CGE and Alsthom have also joined

---

[4] The *Wall Street Journal*, March 16, 1964, and August 4, 1964; the *New York Times* (and other daily papers) on or about July 1, 1964.

[5] There is instead a trade association, The International Electrical Association, London, of which all major European manufacturers are members.

21

hands, through Unelec, in the production of motors, small transformers and low voltage equipment. In all these mergers the pressure in France from Electricité de France, and in Britain from the Industrial Reorganisation Corporation, was the significant element. In Italy, Ansaldo San Giorgio, a state-owned manufacturer of heavy electrical equipment, merged its operations with CGE (an Italian subsidiary of General Electric, USA) under the new name of ASGEN. In Austria, there have been numerous bids by foreign competitors to take over ELIN Union, which is itself a merger of ELIN A.G. and AEG-Union. In Switzerland (1967), the Brown Boveri group took over the Maschinen Fabrik Oerlikon with sales of about $40 million and employment of 4,500. Finally, even in Germany, Siemens and AEG-Telefunken have announced that as from April 1, 1969, they will develop, produce and sell jointly their heavy electrical equipment in two jointly-owned subsidiaries (though both will continue to develop nuclear reactors).[6]

International Manufacturing Arrangements

National markets reserved for domestic producers

The internal markets of exporting countries, in most cases, are heavily protected nearly to the point of complete exclusion of imports. First, there is tariff protection ranging from 10 to 20 percent, or higher in some cases.[7] Secondly, each industrial country has its own standards with respect to operational conditions and safety, equipment producers accustomed to working with a given standard and with existing purchasing habits are thus favored. Finally, and perhaps most important, power companies tend to support their domestic industries and usually do not even invite foreign producers to quote. Export and import figures given in Annex Table 2 and consumption figures in Table 2 also support this point. Prices quoted by American manufacturers in the USA (e.g. T.V.A. biddings) have been substantially higher than international prices. This is made possible in part through the Buy American Act.

---

[6] *The Economist*, November 2, 1968; *Der Spiegel*, No. 45 of 1968.

[7] Even in the case where the tariff is insignificant, the import is apparently restricted by the purchaser's preference. For instance, in Switzerland import duties for large hydroelectric generators amount at present to 2.7 to 2.8 percent and for large transformers at about 2.5 percent ad valorem. Imports originating in EFTA countries are exempt from duty. Yet heavy electrical imports into Switzerland are very minor (less than 10 percent of the demand) though standards are identical to those in Continental Europe. This phenomenon cannot be explained only by the price competitiveness of the domestic manufacturers; there may be some elements of purchaser's preference.

Attempts to extend the domestic markets internationally

Three circumstances have facilitated the extension of protected domestic markets beyond national borders:

a) Special relationship with a developing country arising from previous political association, such as language, education and experience of administrators and engineers, existing equipment and trade channels, etc. Against this, it is the policy of some governments to loosen economic ties with former mother-countries. In spite of this policy and in spite of severe competition from continental European and Japanese companies, the British industry is still by far the largest supplier in the Commonwealth countries, though its share may have decreased.

b) The role of consultants hired by the developing country, who are more familiar with the equipment of their home country than with competing equipment from other countries.

c) Tied aid and bilateral agreements. Prices under such arrangements tend to be similar to home market prices in the exporting country, i.e. considerably higher than prices in the free market. Some companies (mainly from Germany and France) disagree that tied aid has an effect on the price. They argue first that international competition exists between supplying countries for both equipment and credits and that beneficiary countries can select both the equipment and the credit terms that suit them best among a generally wide range of proposals. Secondly, they say there will be a number of firms from the donor country participating in tendering, thus ensuring competition. There is reason to doubt whether this does ensure competition, however. General experience is that prices quoted in tenders restricted by a "tied aid competition" are much higher than those in worldwide open competition. In one particular case, even though badly in need of foreign exchange, the purchaser switched from tied-aid procurement to own financing because the price was excessive. It is also argued that the low prices sometimes obtained under competitive bidding are to some extent made possible by higher prices obtained through tied-aid procurement, and in some cases, through high prices in home markets. Heavy equipment producers are natural supporters of bilateral aid programs. It is suggested that without tied aid, competitive prices would tend to rise. But this argument assumes that all exporters are equally efficient and none are currently sheltered by tied aid. Faced with increasing competition in third markets, US manufacturers have compensated by concentrating on sales to developing countries under tied-aid arrangements.

Licensing agreements in the heavy electrical equipment industry are so widespread that every major firm is a licensor and a licensee at the same time. Even among the large firms, only very few have a positive balance of license payments.

In standard light equipment (e.g. motors and distribution transformers), the basic technology and manufacturing procedures are well known and could be copied. Nevertheless, leading manufacturers have experience of great value to newcomers, and introduce many refinements both in products and production techniques which can form the basis for license agreements. A typical fee in this area would be about two to three percent of the value of the output.

Heavy equipment requires skilled design work and time-consuming engineering. In this area newcomers cannot progress without a license and without a continuing working relationship with an established producer. Hence, license fees are higher. From an average of perhaps four to five percent of the product value, they may reach ten to twelve percent on large steam turbines. High license fees are, of course, the reward for successful research and development which has placed a company, at least temporarily, in a unique position in the field.

Many international companies would prefer to sell licenses without getting involved in direct investment and production abroad. This, for many years, was the policy of Westinghouse Electric of the USA with respect to the European market. But policies such as these were disrupted by the firm resolve of several countries to build their own electrical equipment industries. Some companies had established particularly close contacts with certain developing countries, and were induced to help in initiating manufacturing operations in those countries both by their interest in preserving a market and by the pressure of their distributors or manufacturing licensees for light equipment. As manufacturing of heavy equipment was extended to industrializing countries, a need was felt for assistance and supervision of a degree which can only be achieved by participating in management and in equity. At the same time some developing countries insisted on equity participations by the foreign licensor as a condition for permission to manufacture.

Partly as a result of these trends, there are substantial shareholdings by foreign companies, General Electric (United States), Alsthom and GCE (France), Brown Boveri (Switzerland), ASEA (Sweden), Siemens and AEG (Germany), in the Spanish electrical equipment industry. General Electric and Brown Boveri are the major producers in Brazil but ASEA, Siemens, and AEG are also manufacturing there. In Argentina, the principal producers are CEGELEC (financial participation by CGE France) and

24

SIAM Electro-Mecanica (Westinghouse 40 percent). Mexico's major producer is IEM, in which Westinghouse has a leading participation. General Electric, Mexico, is primarily in the light end of the business; there are no other large producers of heavy electrical equipment. In India, three foreign firms, including AEI (United Kingdom), are among the major manufacturers of transformers. It has been the Indian Government's policy for the state to enter the production of heavy generating equipment and heavy traction and industrial equipment. In Pakistan, which is just starting to produce heavy equipment, two out of four dominant electrical equipment manufacturers are Pakistani-owned with license agreements; the other two have foreign majority participations—Siemens (Germany) and Johnson & Phillips (UK).

IV

THE INDUSTRY IN DEVELOPING COUNTRIES

Growth of the Industry

The heavy electrical equipment industry in the developing countries is the outcome of two sets of factors. The first set consists of Government policies favoring the creation of capital goods industries. The second is the interest of international firms in keeping a foothold in every important market as long as possible, which is explained in part by excess plant capacity in the home country and high technical overhead costs.

Governments have shown their vital concern in the creation of this industry by giving it a prominent place in their development plans (e.g. India's second and Pakistan's third plans), and by encouraging private investment through protection, preference in public purchases, or even financial assistance. Because of the know-how required to build custom-designed products of great technological sophistication, the developing countries could not start the industry without the assistance of international concerns. Even in the one case where a wholly-owned government plant was built (the Bhopal plant in India), the purchase of know-how and even managerial assistance from foreign companies was necessary. Governments desired quick forceful action in the hopes of achieving industrial adulthood and of radically cutting import bills. Being unfamiliar with the industry, some of them tended to press too hard for a telescoped increase in capacity with too many producers.

The international companies were taken by surprise, and their first moves were essentially defensive. In the extreme case, they looked upon manufacturing activity as a façade behind which exports could go on in the traditional way. At best, they were skeptical about the return from manufacturing investments; their profits would come instead from license fees and from sales of such parts and components as could not yet be made in the developing country. These profits, of course, would be increased if it were possible to capture the markets of those competitors who were unwilling to come in, or were too late in establishing a manufacturing base. Almost without exception, the international firms question the economics of heavy electrical equipment manufacture in developing countries. Theoretically, if they had realized the determination of the developing countries to build these industries, they might have devised some scheme for sharing the markets rationally and setting up plants at a few selected locations in the developing world. Such a solution, however, was ruled out equally by their own rivalries and by the ambitions of each developing country to possess its own industry.

The disorganized background of the industry and the scramble by the many previous suppliers to defend or capture protected markets explain the present characteristics of the heavy electrical equipment industry in developing countries—small size plants, high cost operations and doubtful growth prospects. With a longer history of protection, the Spanish industry in some ways provides an exception to this rather discouraging pattern.

Country Experiences

Spain

The Spanish heavy electrical equipment industry achieved large output during World War II and was given a rapid boost by intensified power development after the war. More recently, railway electrification and industrial expansion have helped to increase sales. International companies, including General Electric, Westinghouse, Alsthom, CGE, and after the war, Brown Boveri, Siemens and ASEA, entered either alone or in joint ventures with domestic firms. As a result, standards improved steadily, and there was no significant technological lag.

At the present moment, the main producers are General Eléctrica Española (General Electric, United States, has now acquired a dominant interest), which probably accounts for about one-half of the total domestic production, and Cenemesa (a Westinghouse licensee), which may account for another quarter. La Maquinista, a major Spanish equipment producer, makes generators and motors for diesel electric locomotives and is preparing to make turbo-alternators for thermal power stations under a license from Brown Boveri, Switzerland, an important shareholder. Other producers make mainly transformers and motors.

The Government has facilitated the industry's growth by import controls and protective duties. Duties are generally high on light equipment (50 percent, plus 10 percent on induction motors) but somewhat lower (20 to 25 percent, plus 5 percent) on heavy equipment. Until recently, import licensing was quite restrictive and was as important as the tariff in protecting the domestic industry. Nevertheless, there has been a gradual and efficient growth in the capability of the industry and in domestic content.[1]

The Spanish industry does not appear to have suffered from those drastic changes in equipment purchases by the local power industry which have been a disruptive influence in several of the other countries studied. Prices for electric power have been set so as to facilitate self-financing by power companies, and protection has reserved the market for the domestic industries. In recent years, nevertheless, there has been a sharp upturn in imports of electric power machinery and switchgear—from about $13 million equivalent in 1961 to $32 million equivalent in 1965. This reflects both the increasing importance of thermal power equipment (with a large import component) and the full order books of the Spanish industry.

The Spanish industry has taken full advantage of existing tariff protection, and is not competitive with world market prices. Its main problem is adjusting to rapid changes in technology and size of equipment. This is accentuated by the world market price structure (relatively high prices on new equipment and specialties, against low prices on equipment with well-documented technology and manufacturing techniques) and by the increasing shift in Spain from hydropower to large thermal power stations.

Though domestic demand is sufficient to permit full capacity utilization in most heavy electrical equipment plants, there is an increasing interest in exports, particularly to Latin America. Spanish electrical equipment manufacturers have joined with United States and Canadian manufacturers for the supply of diesel-electric locomotives to Argentina and Brazil. These orders have been facilitated by special trade agreements between Spain and these Latin American countries and by the United States and Canadian financing. The international companies do not seem averse to assigning Spain an export role within their international corporate framework on items or components which can be made cheaply in that country.

---

[1] Present capabilities and domestic content for all the countries studied are summarized in the last section of this chapter.

Brazil is similar to Spain in having a large power market; the annual growth in electric generating capacity exceeds one million kw. As in Spain, most of the present demand can be met through hydropower, but whereas in Spain thermal power seems to be gaining ground in new orders, in Brazil reliance on hydropower will be possible for many years. Another difference is that in Spain the industry grew steadily, while the growth in Brazil was explosive; the share of imports in the total consumption of heavy electrical equipment fell from 94 percent in 1956 to 55 percent in 1964 and to about 33 percent in 1965.

The provenance of the industry dates from 1949, when a commission was formed to study ways of meeting the growing demand for heavy electrical equipment. As a result, several international firms were invited to start manufacturing heavy electrical equipment and were given facilities for duty-free imports of the necessary plant, as well as strong assurances of protection for the finished products.

The first major international producer to establish large-scale manufacture of heavy electrical equipment in Brazil was Brown Boveri, Switzerland. Its Brazilian subsidiary, almost wholly owned, achieved a rapid buildup in capacity during 1958–1962, and in the latter year was equipped to design and manufacture practically every type of rotating equipment. The only other company with a similar broad capability is General Electric S.A., a subsidiary of General Electric, United States. This company, which had been manufacturing light and medium electrical equipment for years, started operations in its new heavy equipment plant in 1962. Other major foreign firms, like ASEA, Siemens and AEG, have also initiated manufacturing operations in Brazil, as yet primarily for power transformers.[2]

The Brazilian industry is capable of producing power equipment up to voltages of 500 kv, although its present experience is limited to 70 Mva for generators and 70 Mva for power transformers as a three phase unit. Heavy switchgear and heavy duty motors are not yet produced. The import component may range from less than 10 percent for a 15 Mva generator or 700 hp synchronous motor to 30 percent for a 33 Mva transformer or a 50 Mva generator. Imported inputs include copper, grain-oriented silicon steel, mica, bushings over 60 kv, and some types of insulating paper. Automatic tap changers for transformers and regulators for generators are also imported as are certain castings and forgings outside the capacity of the Brazilian industry.

---

[2] Siemens has also delivered some large hydroelectric generators produced in their local factory.

The most important problem faced by the industry was the recruitment of staff at all levels. Although the industrial environment of São Paulo was highly favorable, the creation of the electrical equipment industry coincided with unparalleled growth and expansion of the mechanical and automotive industries and the steel industry. Craftsmen capable of operating production machinery were scarce, as were engineers and draftsmen. There were also some supply problems. For instance, several firms attempted to manufacture unmolded mica sheets for commutation segments (needed for uniform properties and high heat stability), but the product turned out to be very expensive (up to four times the cost of the imported material, including duties) and, worse, of poor quality. The newly established plants had to operate in an inflationary environment and had difficulties in securing a steady flow of work. Local procurement of heavy equipment has been somewhat erratic, reflecting both economic fluctuations and variations in foreign financing for power loans.

Brazil's heavy electrical equipment industry has not yet reached even the competitive level of the Spanish industry. There have been difficulties in meeting delivery schedules and in spite of relatively high prices, the profitability to date has been low. Yet, the outlook is good, given the capability attained in a short time and the large domestic market; unlike Spain, Brazil will have a market for hydroelectric equipment for many years.

Argentina

In Argentina, the existence of a light electric equipment industry helped to give rise to a heavy industry. Earnings from existing enterprises, which were mostly foreign-owned, were not transferable and had to be invested in the country; severe competition in the light sector also drove firms into the new field of heavy equipment. The industry was given substantial government encouragement, until 1958 by quantitative import restrictions and, more recently, by high duties and import surcharges.

Between 1958 and 1964, domestic production of heavy electric equipment grew rapidly from 1.5 billion pesos to nearly 3 billion pesos at constant 1960 prices. Three firms account for the bulk of the output of heavy electric equipment. CEGELEC, a subsidiary of the French firm CGE, is the oldest manufacturer of heavy transformers in Argentina; it produces mainly power and distribution transformers and also some switching equipment. Electrica Mechanica Argentina was founded in 1952 to make control panels; it has diversified production to include switching equipment. The third major producer, Siam di Tella Electrica Mechanica, was created in 1959, with a participation by Westinghouse of the United States, to manufacture generators, transformers, motors, capacitors, electric traction equipment, etc.

Most firms were originally established, under some government pressure, to manufacture mainly one product (say, transformers or oil field pumps) for which the public sector was the major buyer. When it became clear that public sector orders were very irregular and payments often slow, all companies were forced to diversify their operations in order to achieve a more continuous flow of work. This has led to high capital output ratios and also to an excessive number of producers for each major product.

The industry produces transformers up to 60 Mva and generators up to 8 Mva as well as electric traction equipment and medium switchgear. In addition to heavy equipment, the main companies also produce capacitors, control panels, light switchgear, and several other items.

Excessive diversification, unused capacity, large inventories because of import controls, and difficulties in obtaining outside finance explain the high price level for Argentine heavy electrical equipment. Domestic supplier industries are generally heavily protected and prices are high for copper, semi-manufactures, and for insulation materials. On balance conditions in Argentina in recent years have been so abnormal that one cannot use the past as the basis for future projections of growth and development. Nevertheless, government policies appear to have been wanting in two respects—lack of planning in procurement and excessive protection both of the electrical equipment industry and of its supplier industries.

Mexico

The light electrical equipment industry was launched in the middle 1940's when the Mexican Government began a conscious policy of industrialization. Substantial protection and tax incentives were granted and some important foreign producers were attracted. The industry is still producing mainly light equipment, but one firm, IEMSA, in which Westinghouse Electric, USA, has an important participation, has emerged as a dominant firm in the manufacture of heavy transformers, motors and switchgear. Generators above 30 Mva are not produced locally.

There has been a gradual and efficient buildup of the industry's capacity and, as we shall see later, today's prices for transformers in the 15 to 20 Mva range are competitive by international standards. On the other hand, heavy motors are about 40 percent above the world market price level and light motors (which fall outside this study) are very expensive. In Mexico, prices for major inputs such as silicon steel and copper are still comparatively high. Transformer grade sheets, which are imported, are normally expensive. Furthermore, high protection has encouraged the establishment of industries supplying secondary raw materials of lower than average quality and very high prices by international standards.

Originally, the Mexican industry was faced with a shortage of engineers, draftsmen and skilled laborers, which called for very extensive in-plant training programs for skilled labor and special training of the professional staff abroad. Today, the major problems faced by the industry are said to be excessive fluctuations in government procurement (due to insufficient planning, shortage of funds, etc.) and foreign competition.

India

Unlike the other countries analyzed in this chapter India was not visited for the purposes of this study: the data here are from reports of other visits and from published sources. However, it was felt that the Indian experience was too important to leave out, despite the quality of data on which it is based. The analysis of India's industry has thus to be read with caution. The first transformer factory in India was the Government Electric Factory at Bangalore, built in 1936, which had an output of 6,000 kva before World War II. Only two firms were engaged in the manufacture of electric motors before the war, P.S.G. and Sons, of Coimbatore, and Kirloskar Bros., Ltd., of Kirloskarvadi. Total output was around 1,000 hp. Due to shortages of imported equipment during the war and especially because of the industrialization policies of the Government after independence, the industry expanded its capacity 24 percent per year between 1950 and 1963. However, production has lagged very much behind the growth in production capacity. The Indian experience is probably a unique illustration of the difficulties which may arise from a very fast expansion of output and size of product in the electrical equipment industry.

The private sector of the industry consists of a large number of firms. The number of manufacturers of electric motors increased from 31 in 1958 to 108 in 1962 and 127 in 1963. Over 20 firms produce transformers. Nevertheless, in both transformer and electric motor production four or five firms account for over 60 percent of total output and a much higher proportion of output of heavy equipment. (For a list of the important private manufacturers see Annex Table 14.) These firms, several of which have foreign participations but no foreign majority control, are very small by international standards; the 1962 sales volumes of the five largest manufacturers of transformers ranged between 25,000 kva and 165,000 kva. A representative plant would have about 1,500 employees and a sales volume of Rs 25 to 30 million (US $5 to $6 million equivalent). The most representative type of ownership is a public limited company wholly owned by Indians having a license agreement with a foreign company of international repute, or jointly owned by Indians and foreign companies. There are wholly private and wholly state-owned companies. Sometimes public bodies such as state governments are partners with foreign companies. Several of the international firms, and the Soviet and Czechoslovakian Governments, have collaboration arrangements in manufacturing in India. The distinctive characteristics of this expansion of plant can be explained by the size of the country, the government's plans for expansion of power generation, regional differences, and high profits in spite of low plant utilization.

When imports of electrical equipment into India were curtailed, new operations were started by Indian and foreign companies, who had been attracted by the Government policy towards industrialization and by what appeared to be a promising new market. Continental European and US products had played little part in the Indian market prior to independence, and the opportunity which suddenly opened must have appeared difficult to resist. The size of the population indicated a potentially good market but information about income distribution, supplier capabilities, availability of skilled manpower and managerial capability was not well documented. The result was that many operations were hurriedly entered into, poorly planned and wrongly equipped. Supplier capability has remained a problem, and, more important, there have been continuous shortages of raw materials, and inadequate standards in materials and component parts. Many difficulties have now been overcome, and a survey by the Tariff Commission of India indicates that even before the recent devaluation, ex-factory costs in many cases were lower than *c.i.f.* prices of competing imports. For instance, a 250 kva Indian transformer was over 10 percent cheaper and a 1,250 kva transformer was over 15 percent cheaper; prices were about equal or slightly higher for a 5,000 kva transformer. In spite of excess capacity and shortage of imported raw materials, profitability is good; after tax it averaged about 14 percent of net worth in 1964–65.

Low prices for motors and transformers do not necessarily demonstrate competitiveness, however. For instance, in procurement of transformers, low energy losses would also be a major consideration. If all design characteristics are considered, it may be judged that the Indian electric motor and transformer industries have not yet attained full international competitiveness. Improved design would not only assure the consumer better value but would also permit substantial foreign exchange savings on imported materials. In 1965, only about 15 percent of the motors produced in India had die-cast rotors. If these rotors were used universally, copper imports for the production of electric motors could be cut by 20 percent. Similarly, the use of cold-rolled, grain-oriented sheets in transformers, apart from a 10 percent reduc-

33

tion in losses (a tremendous gain) would also yield 10–25 percent savings in the requirements of steel and copper which are the major raw materials. The Tariff Commission of the Government of India suggests that "the long and expensive time lag between the established use of improved design and materials in overseas countries and their acceptance in India is due to the inertia of indigenous producers who enjoy a sheltered market and higher price level for their product."[3] But this "inertia" is itself related to the fact that, in a rigidly controlled economy, competition is thwarted by raw material allocation and the producer has little flexibility for introducing new products or new methods of production.

By concentrating on the heavy side of this industry, the public sector has undertaken a far more difficult task than that which faces private firms. The Indian Government had considered for many years the setting up of a plant to manufacture heavier items than the private sector produced, e.g. generators, electric locomotives, etc. Heavy Electricals Ltd., India, was formed in 1958, and construction was begun at Bhopal of a large plant to manufacture virtually every type of heavy electrical equipment.[4] There were difficulties in utilizing the huge production potential. Though the Government had anticipated losses for a long initial period, the actual losses were much larger than expected and foreign exchange savings almost negligible. The total investment in Bhopal up to March 31, 1964 was about Rs 600 million (then US $125.4 million) almost equal to the total capital employed of Rs 604 million in the private sector in 1964–65.[5] Though the value of annual output is planned to reach Rs 310 million (then US $64.8 million) eventually, it was only Rs 45 million (US $9.5 million) in 1963–64. The Bhopal plant has had difficulties in starting up but these difficulties may be overcome in time. It will be far more difficult to offset the effects of excessive diversification and high overheads.

Despite this unpromising beginning, in 1963 and 1964 construction was begun on three new heavy electrical equipment plants, and Bharat Heavy

---

[3] Report of the Tariff Commission on Protection of Electric Motors, 1963.

[4] This was contrary to the advice of consultants (1953) who had concluded that the production of heavy electrical equipment in India would be an uneconomic proposition. If the Government felt that the national interest dictated the construction of such a plant, independently of economics, they suggested the following alternatives to be adopted singly or together: a) to develop the single line of manufacture which appeared to offer the greatest chance of being an economic venture, namely traction equipment, and/or b) to take over an existing factory and expand its operation as and when it became economically practicable.

[5] These figures are for all the operations and output of the 21 largest private firms (including their light equipment manufacture). All dollar values are at the pre-1966 parity rate of $1 = Rs 4.7619.

Electricals Ltd. was incorporated as a separate public manufacturing enterprise to administer these three units. Total final investment is estimated at Rs 1,310 million (then US $276 million) with projected sales of Rs 760 million (US $160 million). Partial production has begun, and capacity production in all three plants is scheduled for 1970–71.

According to the Bureau of Public Enterprises in India,[6] the High Pressure Boiler Plant, Tiruchirapalli, which has Czech technical and financial assistance, is designed for the manufacture of high pressure boilers equivalent to 750 MW. The plant will employ 6,000 people when full production is reached. The Heavy Power Equipment Plant, Hyderabad, is also being developed with Czech assistance. The plant is designed to manufacture steam turbines, turbo-alternators and pumps equivalent to an output of 800 MW per annum in sizes up to 100 MW each. A separate switchgear unit is also being undertaken in collaboration with ASEA of Sweden. The employment potential is 4,350. Heavy Electrical Equipment Plant Hardware has Soviet assistance to manufacture steam turbines and turbo alternators in ranges of 50 to 200 MW hydro-turbines and generators of unit sizes up to 100 MW, and large A.C. and D.C. motors.

Pakistan

There was practically no manufacture of electrical equipment in Pakistan prior to partition. Independence led to some manufacture but growth during the 1950's was relatively slow and mainly concentrated on light equipment (fans, low-tension switchgear, light motors and distribution transformers). In the early 1960's Pakistan entered a new phase as a result of deliberate government policy. New protective tariffs for motors and transformers were published in 1961–62, and the private development bank, PICIC, financed investments to the extent of about $2 million equivalent in investment credits.

There are nine producers of electrical equipment in Pakistan but most of their production is in items falling outside our definition of heavy electrical equipment (distribution transformers, light motors, low-tension switchboards, etc.) With one or two exceptions, the major units have been started by foreign capital or with the aid of foreign partners (Siemens, Johnson & Phillips, AEG, English Electric).

The increase in output of major items was quite dramatic, as may be seen from the following summary:

---

[6] *Annual Report on the Working of Industrial and Commercial Undertakings of the Central Government, 1964–1965*, Bureau of Public Enterprise, Government of India.

Value of output, $ million equivalent, current prices

	1956–57	1962–63	1964–65
Transformers	0.28	1.2	4.0
Motors	0.06	0.3	2.3
Switchgear	0.10	1.3	2.8
Total	0.44	2.8	9.1

In 1965, domestic production covered about 60 percent and 50 percent respectively of the demand for motors and transformers. Output was as yet on a very small scale; the largest manufacturer of transformers had an output of about $1 million equivalent, while the largest manufacturer of motors produced less than 2,000 motors, worth only about $250,000. In terms of capabilities, the industry produced a range of 11/0.4 kv transformers up to 1,500 kva, motors up to 50 hp, switchgear of 11 kv, with a maximum rating of 350 Mva. Even though Pakistan's total production of heavy electrical equipment was not far below $10 million equivalent in 1965, imports of power machinery rose from $15 million equivalent in 1961 to $21 million equivalent in 1965. Aided by the Government's export incentive program, the Pakistan industry has received an important export contract for switchgear to Kuwait and a smaller order for switchgear to Australia.

The Pakistan industry is not, as yet, nearly competitive. Prices for motors, transformers, and switchgears are generally 25 to 35 percent above the equivalent *c.i.f.* price of imports. As we shall see presently, raw and semi-finished material costs (except for iron castings) are 40 to 60 percent or more above Western European levels. The scale of production is small for the types of items presently produced, capacity utilization is low (generally one shift only), and inventories are extremely high, reflecting fears of a cut-off from imported supplies. The industry suffers from a shortage of technical and management skills, and there are instances of friction with overseas partners. Pakistan is a relatively small market; the installed capacity in 1965 was only 1,150 MW in five systems which were not interconnected, and which used a variety of generating equipment (hydro, steam, and gas turbines). The desirable lines of future development of the industry therefore are far from clear, and would merit a special study.

Capabilities

The industries in the six countries studied, except Spain, were established during the last decade. In all six countries, they have achieved the capability of

36

supplying the bulk of the distribution equipment. Capacities for heavy power generation and transformation are shown in Table 6.

TABLE 6: **The Maximum Size of Equipment Being Built by Domestic Manufacturers, 1967**

(Mva)

Country	Power Transformers (3 phase)	Generators	
		Hydro	Thermal
Spain	200	255	81
Brazil	70	70	–
Argentina	60	8	–
Mexico	100	–	–
India	75	37	–
Pakistan	2	–	–
Portugal	150	–	–

Sources: Portugal, 20th Report, 1967, *op. cit.*; Spain, General Eléctrica Española, see Figure 1; others, interviews with manufacturers, 1966. The results differ from those given in Annex Table 4 because of the different sources.

All the countries listed except Pakistan can supply most of the power transformers needed; Brazil and Spain have the capability of producing transformers up to 400 kv. In generating equipment, where the learning period is the longest, Spain has produced hydroelectric generators of 255 Mva. The Alcantara Storage Plant is to be equipped with four 200 MW generators, the largest hydro units in Europe. Brazil has produced 70 Mva hydroelectric generators, and could build 150–200 Mva units. India has produced 40 Mva units. In contrast, Argentina has built only small units and Mexico none. Only Spain has built thermal generating equipment; the industry there is preparing to produce units above 100 Mva.

The pace of growth of capability is as important as the limits of capability actually reached. It took the Spanish industry about seven years to move from hydraulic generators of 2.4 Mva (1952) to 29 Mva (1959) and another seven years to reach 255 Mva (1966). (See Figure 1, p. 38.) Very similar progress can be seen in Brazil. In 1958, the upper limit of generators built was 4.3 Mva; it rose to 50 Mva by 1965. Today, the capability is about 150 to 200 Mva, though the industry is not as competitive for these large generators as it is for the smaller types.

In discussing capabilities, the domestic component should also be considered. In transformers, the import content is determined more by raw material availabilities than by the technical capability of the industry. In Mexico,

37

FIGURE 1.   Evolution of Size of Vertical Generators, Spain, 1952–66

1952   1953   1956   1959   1961

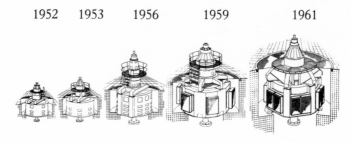

From left to right: Burgomillado (1 unit) 2.4 Mva; Espot (3 units) 6.1 Mva; Bosost (2 units) 13.5 Mva; Pont de Rey (2 units) 29 Mva; Las Ondinas (2 units) 50.5 Mva.

1962–63   1965–66

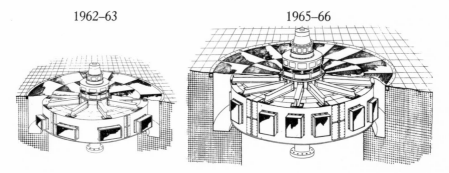

From left to right: Ribarroja (3 units GEE-Alsthom) 84 Mva; Alcantara (4 units GEE-Alsthom) 225 Mva.

where copper is available locally, imported materials represent about 27 percent of the sales price of a transformer while the comparable proportion for Brazil is about 40 percent and for Pakistan over 50 percent. In generators, the import component is generally higher, representing, for instance, two-thirds of the value of a generator produced in Brazil. A substantial reduction of the import component of generators can be achieved if heavy castings and forgings are produced in the country. This is one reason why, in Spain, the domestic industry is now contributing 70 percent of the value of a steam turbine generator set.

V

PRICES FOR HEAVY ELECTRICAL EQUIPMENT

World Market Prices

The intense competition at present in the sale of heavy electrical equipment has had two effects on prices. In the first place, prices for several major types of heavy electrical equipment in most major producing countries have fallen by as much as 25 percent during the last five years, the dip being severe for both thermal generators and power transformers. Secondly, prices quoted on the free world market (outside tied aid and bilateral trade) have generally fallen well below domestic prices in the major producing countries. And, as will be suggested below, there is no indication that world market prices will increase substantially over the next few years.

In this chapter we shall first analyze the structure and major determinants of world market prices for heavy electrical equipment. Secondly, we shall study prices in developing countries and their relationship to world market prices.

The following points are basic to an understanding of the price formation for heavy electrical equipment on the world market:

a) *Relative smallness of world market.* Compared to total sales of heavy electrical equipment, the market subject to competition is relatively small. The French and the German markets are completely closed to outsiders; the United Kingdom market is virtually closed, even to partners in EFTA. Historically, there have been few imports of electrical equipment to the United States, due, in part, to domestic preferences.[1]

b) *Importance of tied aid.* For equipment moving in international trade, there are two price levels. One, applying to tied-aid contracts, is aligned on domestic price levels in the exporting countries. On the free world market, on the other hand, prices quoted are generally below home market prices in major exporting countries.

c) *Impact of excess capacity.* Reference has already been made to the over-capacity in the industry. But the problem of reasonable capacity utilization is, to some extent, present in the industry even in normal times. Because of the long production cycle and the large share of fixed expenses in the total cost, each international firm is anxious at times to capture a particular order which would fill its plant capacity nicely and help keep its key staff and skilled labor occupied. On such occasions, a firm will quote a price designed to secure the order and will forget about the normal profit margin.

d) *Protection.* It cannot be denied that domestic prices are substantially above world market prices. This situation persists because on its home ground each national industry is protected from the full force of international competition.

When discussing world market prices we shall reserve this term for prices quoted in international competitive bidding. Since at any moment a developing country is notionally free (subject to foreign exchange availability) to procure equipment on the world market, this is the standard against which it must judge the economics of domestic production. It has been suggested that free world market prices are not a relevant standard because so much heavy electrical equipment is bought by developing countries under tied aid at considerably higher prices. But first, tied aid could sometimes be switched to some other commodity, and secondly, even if it could not, the higher cost of tied aid is best considered separately, as a price paid for financial resources which would not be forthcoming without it.

There may be many reasons why a company quotes a certain price. The price quoted in the free competition would reflect the long-term business in-

---

[1] The above statements may seem contradictory to the analysis in Chapter III showing that many industrial countries are both exporters and importers of heavy electrical equipment. Nevertheless, judging from our conversations with European manufacturers, imports are largely (though not exclusively) of items not made in the purchasing country. Some German firms did not agree with the statement that their home market is closed and adduced global statistics to support their argument. But if the trade in specialized patented items is excluded, the import of power equipment by power utilities can be shown to be very small indeed. (See Annex Table 2.)

terests of the company related to the work load of the plants and its anxiety to capture a particular job at a particular moment. Firms will often decide their prices on the basis of current costs only, and some may even accept losses in order to break into a new market. There may also be some international or intercompany motives other than economic. Nevertheless, an attempt to analyze prices is made here.

Each large generator or transformer is a unique piece of equipment. A serious study of international prices therefore requires some method of formula by which prices for different sizes of generators may be reduced to a common reference basis. This can be achieved approximately by a) expressing all prices in $ per kva and b) estimating the average relationship between the size of the generator, expressed in Mva/pole, and the price. This has been done in Figure 2 which was supplied by courtesy of an international manufacturer.

In the schedule of bids from which Figure 2 was derived, one may observe price differences of up to 50 percent, or even more, among tenders submitted by international companies for the same job. At first glance, Figure 2 suggests a bewildering anarchy in price formation. Nevertheless, a pattern may be discerned; individual variations from this pattern generally have a rationality of their own. If a producer has already delivered one generator, the buyer may prefer to buy a second generator from the same source, even at some price premium. Or if, on the contrary, it has become strategically important to a certain producer to gain production experience for a new (generally heavier) type of generator or transformer not previously made by him, he may be willing to go down in price (though, paradoxically, his costs may be unusually high compared to the world market price). Refinements, or special equipment, or difficulties of installment may justify a slightly higher price. Finally, unsettled financial or political conditions in a given country may cause producers generally to adjust their bids upward.

Keeping these disturbing elements in mind, one may describe the price formation on the international market roughly as follows. During any given period of time there is a great deal of uniformity in the international price level, and all firms can apparently determine within a range, perhaps as narrow as five percent, what the successful bid will be on a new tender. Many firms would quote high prices, knowing they were high, because not to quote any price (not submitting a tender when they were invited to) might affect future invitations by the same purchasers. Whether a given firm would gear its quotation towards the lower or the higher end of the range would depend upon a series of factors: its desire to stay in touch with a particular market, its competitiveness on a particular type of equipment, the degree to which it faces unused capacity, and its preference for aggressive competition or stability.

42

Normally, however, no firm would quote below the expected range for fear of starting a price war. At some point, nonetheless, some combination of factors listed above may induce an international manufacturer to break below the previous price line, and a new low level will be established. This appears to have happened on at least four different occasions within the last six years (see Figure 2). Developing countries, in trying to become price competitive, are therefore chasing a moving target. Conceptually, in looking for a standard for price competitiveness, we must look for a point or points in time when the world market prices were consistent with their long-run trend. In practice, no such precision is possible.

Our best guess is that world market prices in 1965 were consistent with their long-run trend. We have been told by some producers in industrial countries that these prices were 15 to 20 percent below a level which would have provided them with a normal profit margin. Yet three factors suggest that prices will remain low for some time to come: the large excess capacity in the industry, the further fall in prices since 1965, and, finally, indications that those firms which were most aggressive price-wise and hence filled their order books *did* earn a profit. The strategy of marginal pricing has several facets, and is likely to be practiced even during periods when there is relatively little unused capacity. First, in a world-wide industry even in normal times, some firms are bound to have unused capacity spurring them to marginal pricing. Secondly, assuming that there are advantages from greater volume of sales and that price discrimination (e.g. between home market and exports) is possible, a firm may well plan some capacity for exports. In this sense marginal pricing promotes growth: growth in experience and capability, growth perhaps in more modern facilities.

In conclusion, no developing country should initiate the manufacture of heavy electrical equipment on the implicit assumption that present world market prices are "abnormally low" and therefore likely to increase.

Prices in Developing Countries

There are technical difficulties in comparing prices for heavy electrical equipment in different countries. First, the equipment is not identical: varying technological environment, industrial capabilities, domestic content rules, and purchaser's preferences may cause substantial differences in design and in performance (e.g. in reliability, maintenance requirements, and life expectancies). Secondly, the delivery time and, perhaps most important, the financial arrangements will have a bearing upon the price.

Power companies try to compare bids in different ways. Thus, payment plans may be made comparable by reducing the total prices to present values.

43

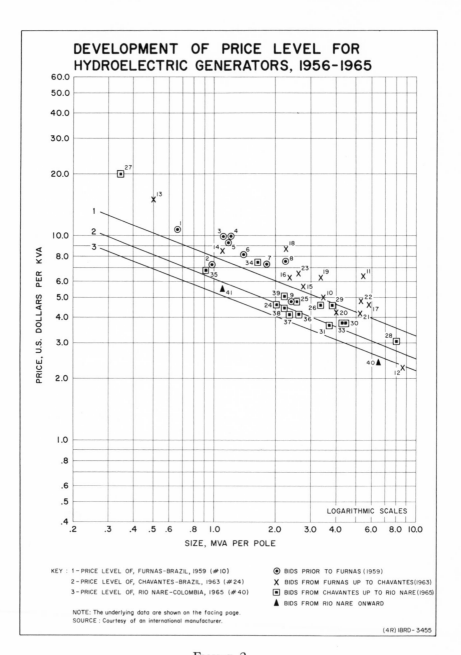

DEVELOPMENT OF PRICE LEVEL FOR HYDROELECTRIC GENERATORS, 1956-1965

PRICE, U.S. DOLLARS PER KVA

SIZE, MVA PER POLE

LOGARITHMIC SCALES

KEY : 1 — PRICE LEVEL OF, FURNAS-BRAZIL, 1959 (#10)
2 — PRICE LEVEL OF, CHAVANTES-BRAZIL, 1963 (#24)
3 — PRICE LEVEL OF, RIO NARE-COLOMBIA, 1965 (#40)

NOTE: The underlying data are shown on the facing page.
SOURCE : Courtesy of an international manufacturer.

⊙ BIDS PRIOR TO FURNAS (1959)
X BIDS FROM FURNAS UP TO CHAVANTES(1963)
▣ BIDS FROM CHAVANTES UP TO RIO NARE(1965)
▲ BIDS FROM RIO NARE ONWARD

(4R) IBRD-3455

FIGURE 2

Legend: Successful Bids—Data Underlying Figure 2

		Mva/Pole	US $/kva
1.	Almus (Siemens) 1959	0.66	10.75
2.	Sefid Roud (Jeumont)	0.98	7.25
3.	Caroni 5/6 (AEG)–60 cycles per second	1.11	9.92
4.	Matahina (English Electric)	1.21	9.92
5.	Rio Macho (Shibaura) 60 c.p.s.	1.17	9.25
6.	Mareta (English Electric)	1.40	8.12
7.	Yanhee (AEG)	1.82	7.25
8.	Salto II (AEG) c.p.s.	2.25	7.50
9.	Calima (Mitsui) 60 c.p.s.	2.40	4.75
10.	Furnas (Siemens) 60 c.p.s. 1959	3.45	5.00
11.	Poatina (Siemens)	5.42	6.39
12.	Murray (ASEA)	8.60	2.24
13.	Cundinamarca (Oerlikon) 60 c.p.s.	0.50	15.00
14.	Brokopondo (Siemens) 60 c.p.s.	1.10	8.50
15.	Volta River (IGE)	2.75	5.66
16.	Rapel (Hitachi)	2.35	6.25
17.	Konya II (AEG)	5.80	4.60
18.	Angat River (ASEA) 60 c.p.s.	2.25	8.65
19.	Furnas (Exp.) Siemens 60 c.p.s.	3.35	6.25
20.	Mangla Dam (Hitachi)	4.00	4.20
21.	El Colegio (ACEC) 60 c.p.s.	5.23	4.15
22.	El Colegio (ASEA) horizontal 60 c.p.s.	5.30	4.75
23.	Maria Christina (Toshiba) 60 c.p.s.	2.60	6.50
24.	Chavantes (Toshiba—ASEA) 60 c.p.s.	2.05	4.62
25.	Paulo Alfonso (ASEA) 60 c.p.s.	2.55	4.74
26.	Cachi (Toshiba) 60 c.p.s.	3.35	4.56
27.	Nam Pong (AEG)	0.345	20.00
28.	Murray III (ASEA)	8.00	3.05
29.	Guri (AEG) 60 c.p.s.	3.80	4.55
30.	Guri (Hitachi) 60 c.p.s.	4.40	3.75
31.	Guri (Westinghouse) 60 c.p.s.	3.70	3.65
32.	Awash II and III (Elin)		
33.	Manapouri (Siemens)	4.30	3.75
34.	Corani (Siemens)	1.65	7.45
35.	Cumbaya (AEG) 60 c.p.s.	0.91	6.75
36.	Kovada II (AEG)	2.60	4.12
37.	Blowering (AEG)	2.35	4.10
38.	Yanhee III–IV (AEG)	2.22	4.40
39.	Yanhee V (AEG)	2.22	5.01
40.	Rio Nare (AEG) 1965	6.50	5.50
41.	Aviemere (Siemens)	1.10	5.50

Differences in power losses for transformers may be capitalized in a similar manner. Nevertheless, some element of guesswork or judgment is inevitable for certain estimates, e.g. the future loading pattern, duration of service, discount rate, etc. Our findings on comparative prices can only be crude approximations, though it is our hope that through cross-checks with manufacturers participating in the study, we have avoided gross errors of fact or judgment.

We also encountered two major analytical difficulties:

a) In some countries, the exchange rates in effect at the time of our comparison were misleading because import duties and other import restrictions were used not only for infant industry protection but also as a substitute for devaluation. Though this aspect was present to some extent in several of the countries studied, it was a major factor in Argentina and required the adjustment described in Annex A.[2] Some adjustments also had to be made in the case of Brazil.

b) It was difficult to establish what point of the "learning curve" each country had reached. This is discussed in Chapter VII. The implications of, say, a 20 percent price difference are very different for an industry clearly in an infant stage, and for one which has had time to acquire the necessary production experience. Differences in domestic content and in the sizes and capacities of equipment should be considered when comparisons among developing countries are made.

The following table summarizes the available price information. It in-

TABLE 7: **Price Premia for Electrical Equipment in Developing Countries Compared with World Market Prices, 1964**

(*percent*)

	Spain	Brazil	Mexico[a]	Argen- tina	India	Pakis- tan
Heavy equipment						
Generators	24	30–60		50		
Transformers 40 Mva and above		50	40 (80)	40	75	
Motors, 3-phase, 100–200 hp			65			
High-voltage accessories			70			
Transformers, 5 Mva			10 (40)			
Light equipment						
Transformers, 200–1,500 Kva		25		45	36	44
Motors, 2–20 hp			95		78	77
Switchgear, up to 35 kv				15		

[a] Figures in parentheses indicate the approximate price differential in Mexico four years earlier, in 1960.

---

[2] Our adjustment is only a working hypothesis subject to critique and refinement. Yet we found it the most meaningful method available for comparing Argentine costs and prices with those of other countries.

cludes prices for some light equipment where these are more representative of the present capability and production experience of the country .

The Mexican experience in *transformers* is particularly interesting. Figure 3 shows that Mexican prices for 5 to 15 Mva transformers fell from

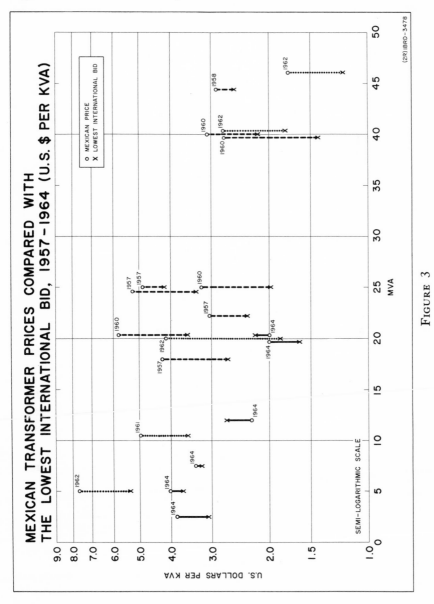

FIGURE 3

47

1.4 to 1.6 times the lowest international bid in 1960 to only about 1.0 to 1.2 times that price in 1964. (In some tenders, Mexican bids were below the international price.) Increased competitiveness may have been due, in part, to a lowering of the Mexican profit margin (present prices do not fully cover costs), but the major factor was probably increased production experience. Brazil shows a similar trend. In bids for 20 Mva and 112 Mva transformers for the Jupia power plant (1962), Brazilian prices were 100 and 120 percent, respectively, above the lowest foreign bid. In the most recent tenders, on the other hand, Brazilian prices have been only 30 to 40 percent above the comparable *c.i.f.* price. The Brazilian prices might be profitable if profit were based upon marginal costs; on an average basis, however, to earn a reasonable return on the investment, Brazilian transformer manufacturers today would probably need prices 50 percent above the world market level.[3]

Generator prices are very much influenced by the size of the domestic component. For two 50 Mva generators for the Chaventes power plant in 1963, Brazilian offers based upon a 15 percent domestic content were only about nine percent above the international price. Yet, based upon a 90 percent domestic content, Brazilian offers were more than twice the lowest foreign bid. Again, with a 33 percent domestic content, Brazilian offers for two 50 Mva generators for the Peixoto power plant (early 1965) were virtually identical with the lowest United States tied-aid bid (say, 25 to 30 percent above the world market price). In a more recent tender, Brazilian prices for one 50 Mva generator were 56 percent above the lowest foreign bid; the price increase apparently reflecting an effort to raise the domestic content to 40 percent or higher. The Brazilian industry has not yet reached the competitiveness of the Spanish industry. With a 45 to 50 percent domestic component, Spanish prices for 100 Mva generators, according to two different sources, are only about 19 to 24 percent higher than domestic prices in France or Austria.[4]

There is an *intermediate range of equipment* for which the competitive disadvantage of manufacturers in the developing countries, at least for some

---

[3] The reader is warned that the price differentials quoted above are not to be taken as indications of a country's comparative advantage in producing heavy electrical equipment. In particular, they may in some cases be inflated by high prices for major materials like silicon sheets or semi-manufactures of copper. The country may have a well established and efficiently run heavy electrical equipment industry but its semi-manufacture industry (like steel) may have some deficiencies. Thus domestic steel prices, which are a major input of heavy electrical equipment, may be much higher than international prices.

[4] The comparison would be somewhat less favorable if made with the world market price *c.i.f.* Spain, since the difference between French domestic prices and the lower French prices for export is greater than the cost of shipping generators from France to Spain.

items, may be less than that for light mass-produced articles or very heavy equipment. These items are produced in relatively small numbers (often to individual specifications) and do not require very powerful manufacturing facilities or very advanced techniques. This intermediate range, the borders of which are not easily defined, includes medium-sized transformers (say, 5 to 20 Mva), and switchgear. Thus, Mexican prices for 10 to 12.5 Mva power transformers are very close to import prices, excluding duty. Argentine prices for switchgear, (other than very heavy switchgear), are only about 15 percent higher than French domestic prices, while Spanish and French domestic prices are virtually identical.

On the other hand, the prices of Mexican-made three-phase 75 to 200 hp *motors* range between 23 and 55 percent above those of imports from the United States, the average being perhaps on the order of 40 percent. (See Annex Table 16.) As a rough estimate, the premium over imports from Europe might be on the order of 65 percent.

A similar situation exists in *high-voltage accessories* where Mexican prices range from 45 to 89 percent above the comparable import price. From interviews with Mexican firms, we found that in 11 cases of pricing for high voltage accessories, the price of the domestic product was:

> 45 to 56 percent higher in 1 case;
> 56 to 67 percent higher in 3 cases;
> 67 to 78 percent higher in 5 cases;
> 78 to 89 percent higher in 2 cases.

Though neither high voltage accessories nor large motors are mass-produced in Western Europe, manufacturers there probably achieve savings by making small production runs for inventory.

Very tentatively, we may summarize the price situation for heavy electrical equipment in developing countries as follows:

a) The first generator or transformer manufactured of a size beyond the previous production experience will be expensive: probably the cost will be 50 percent or more above imports from Western Europe or Japan.

b) As more experience is gained, this premium may be reduced to, say, 20 to 25 percent—the case of Spain. At this stage, competitiveness will depend very much upon the size of the domestic content (beyond 50 percent, for instance, prices for generators are likely to rise rapidly), and the increase in prices for major materials and components due to protection.[5]

---

[5] In international tenders, electrical equipment manufacturers often submit two or more bids corresponding to different assumptions about the domestic content.

c) Developing countries will be most competitive on equipment of intermediate size made to special design when the same equipment is not produced in series in the industrialized countries.

The Moving Target

The international prices with which industries in developing countries are trying to compete constitute a moving target, as Figure 2 has already shown. Figure 4 shows price changes for motors, turbo-generators and transformers; the market decline since 1958–59, especially for transformers, is representative of international price trends. Figure 5 traces the price fall in the USA between 1958 and 1963 by size of transformer. The cost per kva is less for the larger transformers, but the price fall has been greatest in the intermediate sizes.

Figures 6 and 7 demonstrate that prices for equipment in the developing countries have also undergone significant declines. They suggest that no one price level curve is valid for all products, but that there is a price pattern generally applicable to the majority of products. The 1964–66 up-trend in Argentina in Figure 6, for instance, can be clearly seen as contrary to a

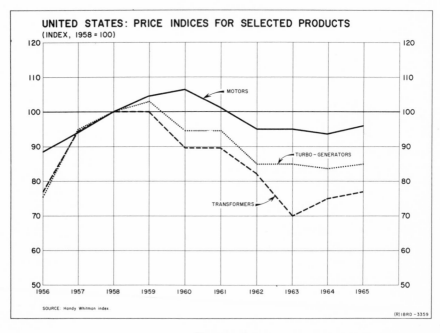

FIGURE 4

50

general declining trend for transformers, which applied to developing country production as well as to the USA.

The effect of the learning process and efforts towards competitiveness of Mexican transformer manufacturers can be seen in Annex Tables 15 and 17. In the years 1957–61 local producers were in competition with the producers from Central Europe; later, from 1962 onwards, they had to face Japanese competition. By 1964 the price ratio of Mexican to foreign bids had markedly improved. For medium-size transformers Mexican producers are now bidding lower than international prices. Figure 8 and Annex Table 18 (from which it is taken) show the competitive position for distribution transformers as it was believed to be in 1965–66. The Mexican price curve per kva is tending to intersect the US curve in the medium-size range.

In the case of motors and special machinery, e.g. in Mexico, prices have not followed the same pattern of decline (Figure 7). This is mainly because production of large motors is relatively new in these countries and also because pricing policies differ. In fixing prices a producer has to decide whether he wants to compete internationally and therefore fix them low, or seek protection and charge higher prices. More detailed information on Mexican motor prices is given in Annex Table 16. It is claimed that the manufacturers

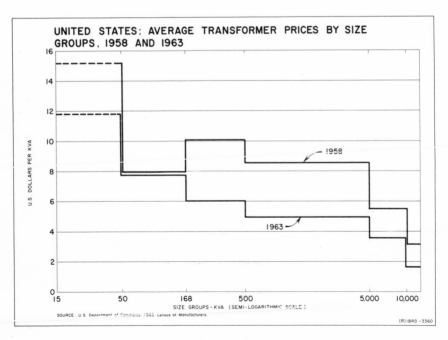

FIGURE 5

51

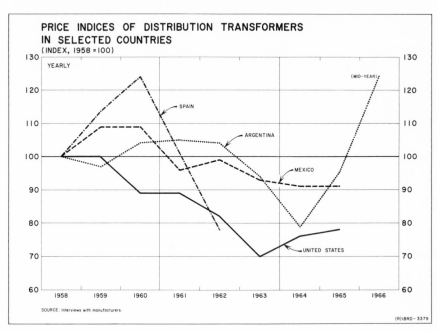

FIGURE 6

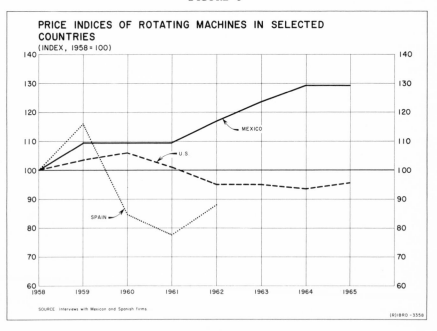

FIGURE 7

52

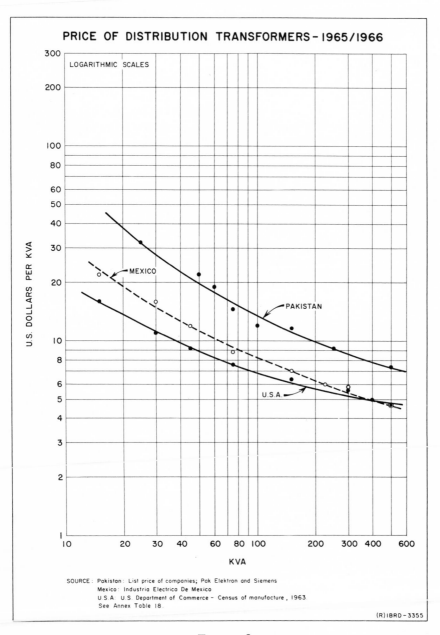

PRICE OF DISTRIBUTION TRANSFORMERS – 1965/1966

LOGARITHMIC SCALES

U.S. DOLLARS PER KVA

MEXICO

PAKISTAN

U.S.A.

KVA

SOURCE: Pakistan: List price of companies; Pak Elektron and Siemens
Mexico: Industria Electrica De Mexico
U.S.A: U.S. Department of Commerce – Census of manufacture, 1963
See Annex Table 18.

(R)IBRD–3355

FIGURE 8

53

in Mexico calculate with a higher profit margin on motors (sold to private industry at protected prices) in order to recoup any fall in the margin on transformers (sold to utilities, and therefore deemed to be more open to "international competition").

Light Industry

Though beyond the scope of the present report, the question is pertinent whether, comparatively speaking, developing countries are in a better position to produce light electrical equipment (e.g. light motors or distribution transformers) than heavy equipment. Table 7 suggests that this would not normally be the case. Figure 8, too, which covers mainly light equipment (transformers in the range below 20 Mva) suggests that there is no comparative advantage for developing countries in this range. The main reason probably lies in the limited size of the market, particularly where a small market is shared by several manufacturers. Where the industry is heavily protected and the domestic content high, manufacture of light equipment, like motors or distribution transformers, is likely to become very uneconomical.

VI

COSTS AND COMPETITIVENESS

ABG

Concepts and Methodology

In this and following chapters we shall compare the costs of producing heavy electrical equipment in developing countries with those in industrial countries. Ideally, we would like to attribute observed cost differences to four major variables:

— factor costs (for materials, manpower, and capital)
— market size
— time and cost of learning process
— institutional framework.

The first three factors taken together determine a country's intrinsic comparative advantage. The fourth factor, the institutional framework, is used as a shorthand phrase for all those conditions, including government policies, which determine whether actual costs exceed costs determined by the country's comparative advantage. For example, government policies might be too protectionist, management-labor relations may be poor, the development of labor and professional skills may have been neglected.

In practice, it is extremely difficult to separate the impact of these different factors. Factor costs depend not only upon the prices and productivity of different factors but also upon their substitutability following changes in tech-

55

nology and the organization of production. The cost disadvantage associated with a small market for, say, hydroelectric generators, might be reduced if the same manpower and the same facilities could be used for production of other items. The length of the learning process will vary with the regularity of orders, which is closely linked with the size of the market but also determined by the institutional framework, e.g. procurement policies.

Faced with these difficulties, we chose the following procedure:

a) In this chapter we compare actual costs,[1] and their major components (materials, manpower, capital);

b) In the next chapter, we discuss the extent to which actual costs have been influenced by market size, the learning process and institutional factors.

Even the comparison of actual costs is not a simple matter. For analytical purposes, we would like to break down each major cost element (materials, labor, capital) into quantities used per unit of production and unit prices. But we are faced with the dilemma that different plants have a different product-mix and, for the same final product, do not perform exactly the same work—some are more fully integrated and make certain components which others purchase from outside. These difficulties we have sought to overcome as follows:

a) In principle, we have taken as our frame of reference the cost structure of firms in Western Europe that are representative of the heavy electrical equipment industry in terms of an individual product or of a firm's total output of heavy electrical equipment.[2] We have then estimated how much the value of each major cost element would deviate in the developing countries from the Western European standard.

b) This comparison is relatively simple for material costs where differences are determined mainly (though not exclusively) by price variations for major materials. On manpower, considerable information is available on relative wages and salaries. Reasonable assumptions regarding the returns on capital in industrial and developing countries can also be made.

c) The real difficulty arises in estimating labor and capital inputs per

---

[1] As distinct from shadow prices. But we make allowances for inflation (see Annex A). Costs of inputs are taken as the manufacturer pays them, and the question of the indirect tax content is not discussed. In a few cases costs will therefore also include import duty on components.

[2] Firms in developing countries seem to be closer to European firms than to American companies, in terms of size, market, and more importantly, product diversification.

unit of output. Though we have some information on individual products for the countries studied, their comparability is suspect and their interpretation exceedingly difficult. We have therefore relied mainly on a different approach. Published profit and loss statements for firms engaged in similar production in Western Europe and in the developing countries have been used to calculate comparative manpower and capital costs per US $ million of sales valued at constant (Western European) prices. This method gives significant results to the extent that the following conditions are fulfilled:

i) the product composition of total sales is reasonably similar;
ii) the degree of vertical integration is reasonably similar;
iii) the conversion of the prices of a given developing country into Western European prices is reasonably correct;
iv) capital costs are properly reported.

It is not necessary that all the above conditions be perfectly fulfilled. For instance, when the product composition or the degree of integration differ, it may be possible to make a rough adjustment for such differences. Moreover, our final estimates have been checked for consistency with some cost comparisons made by international manufacturers between their home and overseas plants. Finally, we have asked the manufacturers participating in our study to check our estimates against their own experiences and such internal cost comparisons as they may have. Even so, in the end, our findings cannot be precise but only broadly suggestive of existing cost differences. And one leading United Kingdom manufacturer has in fact found it impossible to make meaningful comparisons between different plants in the United Kingdom, let alone comparisons with overseas subsidiaries: throughputs would not be comparable, production methods would never be the same, and the proportion of materials and components bought outside would always differ. These are telling points; nevertheless, other manufacturers have tried to make comparisons.

A special study group, International Committee for Economic Comparisons in the Electrical Industry[3] in the European Common Market, has come across similar difficulties while trying to arrive at cost comparisons within the common market countries. The differences in accounting systems seemed to be the major problem. The Committee, therefore, made a special effort to put these on a similar basis in a document called "Guidelines for Calculation of Production Cost in the European Electrical Industry." Students of Amer-

---

[3] Internationaler Arbeitskreis für Betriebswirtschaftliche Vergleiche in der Elektrotechnischen Industrie, *Betriebsvergleiche von Kosten und Kalkulationen*, ZVEI, Frankfurt/Main, 1963.

ican industry report the same kind of difficulties and would agree that the cost data available hardly allow a meaningful comparison. Our approach is different in nature from detailed product comparisons between individual plants. We start out with a measurable difference between domestic prices and world market prices, and then ask ourselves three questions: are material costs higher, are labor costs higher, are charges against capital higher?

Materials

Materials, including processed and semi-finished components, weigh heavily in the cost structure of heavy electrical equipment. In industrialized countries, they generally account for 50 percent or more of the total selling price. The main materials in motors and transformers are copper semi-manufactures and silicon steel sheets; in generators large steel castings are also important. Other important items are insulation materials, porcelain bushings and transformer oil. (See Annex Tables 5 to 8.)

All these materials (except perhaps castings) are normally freely available on the world market. Domestic production therefore is not necessary. In fact, heavily protected domestic production of many of these inputs has sometimes been a major commercial disadvantage to manufacturers in developing countries. They are not always in a position to charge prices for their end products which a) cover the higher cost of domestic materials and/or import duties and b) provide some protection for their processing margin in the learning stage.

A comparison of raw material prices for heavy electrical equipment in developing and industrial countries is given in Table 8 (p. 60). Wire in various forms (blank, enamelled, insulated, etc.) is the dominant copper item for the electrical industry, but other copper products are also used extensively in heavy electrical equipment. The countries studied generally import wire bars which are then turned into semi-manufactures. At present, most copper and brass semi-manufactures cost about 20 to 40 percent more in the three Latin American countries studied than the lowest *f.o.b.* price in the international market. In Pakistan and India, this difference rises to 75 and 100 percent, respectively. The price for drawing copper into enamel wire represents a mark-up of 20 to 30 percent on the cost of bars in Western Europe but of no less than 100 percent in Latin America and Spain.

Due to sharp fluctuations in copper prices and a long-term widening of the price differential between copper and aluminum, the latter metal has been increasingly substituted for copper in industrialized countries, e.g. in small motors. Such substitution has been lagging in developing countries.

The situation for the other main raw material, steel, is interesting. The

58

Brazilian steel industry is almost competitive in ordinary steel sheets. In Mexico, Spain, and Argentina, on the other hand, prices for ordinary sheets are about one-third above the world market level and roughly reflect the present needs for infant industry protection of the domestic steel industries. Spain hopes to be close to international competitiveness in steel when present expansion and modernization plans have been completed by about 1970. The Indian price level reflects the black market prices which are paid for marginal supplies. At the present moment and perhaps for quite some time to come, steel can be imported to any one of the six countries studied at prices, including ocean freight, very similar to those paid in Western Europe and considerably below the prices in the United States. This is because, under present world steel surplus conditions, major steel producers charge considerably lower prices on export sales than on domestic sales.

More important for the industry are the silicon steel sheets of dynamo grade. They are produced in Brazil, Spain, Mexico and India. The price handicap in Spain is about the same as that for ordinary steel sheets. In contrast, prices in Brazil, Mexico and India are almost twice the world market level, reflecting a high level of protection. Transformer-grade, grain-oriented sheets are not produced in the countries studied and with few exceptions their prices are close to the world market level. The high price in Pakistan may be partly the result of tied-aid procurement. The high Brazilian price is explained by a tariff duty, apparently imposed in the hope of inducing domestic production.

Above we have dealt with prices only. We must also consider the quantities of major materials used. The raw material requirements per unit of output in developing countries are larger because of a) higher rejection and working scrap ratios and b) obsolete design. This is therefore another reason for high material costs.

TABLE 8: Prices of Principal Materials, 1966

(lowest f.o.b. price in international trade = 100)

	Prices in the Majority of Advanced Countries[a]	Argentina	Brazil	Mexico	Spain	India	Pakistan
Copper and copper products[b]							
Wire bars	104	123	119	135[c]	128	252	156[d]
Round copper[e]	102	185	136	193	143	188	173
Flat copper	102	n.a.	137	140	133	232	174
Enamelled copper	106	216	159	120	127	194[f]	139
Brass	102	184	n.a.	159	123	168	n.a.
Steel and steel products							
Silicon steel (dynamograde— 3.6 W/kg.—0.5 mm)	115	n.a.	199	196	130	187	167
(Transformer grade grain oriented 0.6 W/kg. 0.35 mm)	108	152[g]	154[h]	112[i]	105[j]	n.a.	123
Steel sheets	106	n.a.	114	130	136	199	150
Hardware	100	n.a.	140	n.a.	135	125	300
Cast iron	106	—	88	150	94	n.a.	69
Insulation material[k,l]	112	140	181[m]	178	190	200	n.a.
Varnish	105	n.a.	n.a.	270	n.a.	168	n.a.
Transformer oil	114	n.a.	98	n.a.	165[n]	190	209

a Even industrial countries do not always buy materials at the lowest prices in the international market. Their home industries produce at higher prices or even if they import from the lowest price sources they have to pay ocean freight, handling and import charges.

b Price comparisons for copper, as far as possible, relate to the situation after the copper crisis. Due to great fluctuations in copper prices, particularly in 1965, the time of purchase has a bearing on the price paid. The price movements were especially harmful to the electrical equipment industries in developing countries. Being in very early stages of production and not large consumers, they had no links with producers and had to purchase copper at the high London Metal Exchange price. In *Argentina*, the unit value of imported unwrought copper (electrolytic copper ingots and slabs) ran fairly close to the LME price—the 1964 unit value was the equivalent of 40 US cents per pound. In addition, the unit value of copper wire imported into Argentina exceeded the unit value of imported unwrought copper by a substantial margin. In November 1965, while industry in advanced countries was paying US $851 a ton for wire bars, Argentine industry had to pay US $1,430 a ton *f.o.b.* (US $1,576 landed), or 185 percent of the international price. *Brazil* imported from Chile at the LME price. The Government and manufacturers tried to establish agreements based on the producers' price but they were not successful. The *Indian* unit import value of unwrought copper ran fairly close to the producers' price in Europe from January to August 1964, but exceeded it by a widening margin thereafter—by the equivalent of about 5 US cents per pound from September to November 1964, 11.5 US cents per pound in December 1964 and 12 to 17 US cents per pound in 1965. Even at its highest, this was well below the LME price, but the price of domestic copper was very high, so the average cost to the industry was considerable. The *Spanish* whole-sale price of unwrought copper, like the Argentine unit import value, ran with the LME price, exceeding it by the equivalent of locally manufactured porcelain for voltages higher than 33 and 69 kv has been poor in practically all countries. The irregular business of the equipment industry does not allow a continuous flow of porcelain bushing imports; therefore there is an important time element involved in the procurement of porcelain bushings for higher voltages. Because of differences in the type of porcelain bushings and their prices, it has been extremely difficult to make an international comparison. One example, however, may serve as an illustration:

Porcelain bushings (SPM – 3241 – 04200 A DIW 42531)

Germany	100
Brazil	235

The Brazilian price is made up as follows: (cost of import $f.a.s.$ = 100)

License charges and others	15.0
Freight	5.6
Insurance	1.1
Banking expenses	6.7
Customs duty	97.1
Importation expenses	8.9
Total	135.3

m Kraft paper in thickness from .0012" is locally available. Electrical (neutral) grades are made by several paper mills up to 100" in width or slightly more. There are no quality problems. Nevertheless, these papers are not made for inventory stock and it is relatively difficult to obtain quantities of less than 10 metric tons per order. Some simple glass fabrics are locally made using imported glass yarn. The maximum width is 6". Cost is competitive with imported equivalents. Glass cloth larger than 6" is imported.

n The reason why transformer oil is excessively high in Spain may be monopolistic pricing.

Note: The international price (= 100) represents the lowest $f.o.b.$ price in the international market (information made available by courtesy of international manufacturers).

some 10 to 12 US cents per pound. At present (1969), since the Zambian Government levies taxation on copper at the LME price, the producers have been constrained to retreat from the double pricing system.

c Copper is produced in Mexico.

d High prices for copper in Pakistan were due mainly to small lot size purchases and tied aid.

e This refers to insulated blank soft copper wire of small diameter. The thickness of wires and also its treatment considerably affect price differences.

f If allowance is made for the low quality of Indian enamelled wire, the price difference would be substantially greater.

g The price difference is mainly due to charges levied on imports. The composition of price was as follows (January 1965)— freight 3.6 percent, import charges 49 percent.

h Silicon steel has been imported at international prices. The price of silicon steel imported from the USA was $535 per ton whereas from Europe it could be imported at $409 per ton. Import charges on silicon steel total around 55 percent.

i The Mexican price includes ocean freight and handling (5.7 percent of $f.o.b.$ value) plus charges and expenses related to import (5.8 percent).

j Based upon a comparison with the German industry for 1963 and 1964.

k In many developing countries the procurement of insulation material presents serious difficulties mainly because of poor quality of domestic production and high protection. As an example of the protection granted to domestic suppliers a summary of import expenses for Brazil is given below (percent of $f.a.s.$ value):

License and other expenses	6.7%
Freight	10.7%
Insurance	0.9%
Banking expenses	6.1%
Financial expenses	3.7%
Customs duty	70.4%
Importation expenses	9.4%
Total	107.9%

l One of the most important items causing serious difficulties in developing countries is porcelain bushings. The quality of

Manpower costs will depend upon a) the cost of the average man-year and b) the manpower requirements per unit of output. Wages and salaries are, of course, much lower in developing countries than in industrial countries, as shown by the following figures for heavy electrical equipment plants:

TABLE 9: Comparison of Wages and Salaries, including All Supplementary Benefits, 1965[a, b]

Country	Absolute Figures		Indices		Ratio Salaries to Wages[c] (*averages*)
	Wages US \$/hour	Salaries US \$/month	Wages	Salaries	
Germany	1.25	305	100	100	1.39
Spain	0.51	213	41	70	2.38
Brazil	0.40	189	32	62	2.70
Japan	0.39	125	31	41	1.84
India	0.25	94	20	31	2.15
Pakistan	0.20	116	16	38	3.31

[a] Also see Annex Table 10 for 1965 data on some countries.
[b] The figures are averages for a representative group of jobs, both at the staff and at the workman level. Hence, they are not influenced by differences in the composition of the workforce. Federal Germany has been chosen to represent industrial countries.
[c] Assuming an average 175 hours per month for workmen in all the countries.
Source: Data submitted by international manufacturer.

According to the table, wages in West Germany are five to six times those in India or Pakistan and about three times those in Japan or Brazil. Differences in salaries are considerably less. German salaries are 2.5 to 3.0 times those in India, Pakistan, or Japan, but only 1.5 to 1.6 times salaries in Spain or Brazil. The relatively low ratios in developing countries reflect primarily the relative surplus of workers. To a lesser extent, they reflect the scarcity of highly skilled staff and of high level administrators who can find employment anywhere and have an international market price. Where foreign personnel are employed, these would normally receive higher pay in developing countries than in their home countries.

Even allowing for the smaller gap in salaries, the sizeable difference in pay scales would seem to give developing countries a competitive advantage in the labor component of cost. In industrial countries, this component accounts for up to 40 percent of the total selling price. Large equipment is virtually handmade, and after the initial learning period, operating times for a given production machine are said to be the same in a country like Brazil as in, say, Sweden. Nevertheless, the extent to which this potential advantage can become a real advantage will depend upon the organization of production, the scale of output, the utilization of plant capacity, etc.

Comparisons of manpower productivity are extremely difficult. The average composition of the output is not the same. The proportion of work done outside the heavy electrical equipment industry varies. Finally, different manufacturing steps and processes will call for different skills and different investment per worker.[4]

Nevertheless, there is enough evidence to suggest that differences in productivity are very large:

a) *Direct labor.* Annex Table 9 indicates that direct man-hour requirements for a range of heavy items were two to three times higher in Mexico and Brazil than in industrial countries. For small motors (light equipment), the difference was even greater; because of the larger scale of output in industrial countries, production can be more mechanized and automated.

b) *Indirect labor.* The proportion of indirect labor tends to be high in developing countries. This category includes, in particular, production of jigs and fixtures, plant maintenance, etc.

c) *Staff.* The staff-to-worker ratios in the SIAM plant in Argentina, the General Electric plant in Brazil or the IEM plant in Mexico are not too different from, say, those at the ASEA works at Ludvika or the Alsthom works at Belfort—about 0.55. The ratio of 0.62 for the Brown Boveri plant in Brazil is somewhat higher; more design work is probably done in this plant. The similarity of the ratios suggests that relatively low productivity is characteristic of staff as well as of workers. One explanation is the need for close supervision in developing countries.[5]

The following figures for manpower costs per US $ million of sales at constant prices clearly suggest that low wage and salary scales in developing

---

[4] Labor productivity also influences material and overhead costs. Low productivity may express itself in more rejects, repairs, or other supplementary work. One manufacturer in Brazil recalled that none of the transformers built in the first three years of operation passed the work tests. Many additional manhours were required to improve the equipment already built.

[5] For light equipment involving a high proportion of standard items, the ratio of staff to workers can be drastically reduced, particularly if no special design capacity is needed and the sales work is routine. For this type of equipment ratios of 0.25 or lower are quite typical. One company in Pakistan producing small motors and transformers in 1958–1960 had a ratio of staff to workers of about 0.08 which was reduced to about 0.05 by 1965. This company lives on purchased or copied technology. When a company develops its own design potential, the ratio is bound to increase.

countries were more than offset by lower productivities.[6] Figures are also shown for employment per $ million of sales.[7] Since the product composition and the degree of out-of-plant work vary, these are not exact measures of productivity; nevertheless we believe that the general picture is fairly conveyed.

TABLE 10: Employment and Manpower Cost against Sales, Heavy Electrical Equipment Industry, Seven Countries

	Employment per $ Million of Sales		Ratio of Manpower Cost to Sales		
	At actual prices	At W. Europe prices[a] ('000 manhours)	At actual prices	At W. Europe prices	Index W. Europe = 100
United States	52	–	.323	–	–
France	92	92	.268	.268	100
Spain	159	176	.347	.396	148
Brazil	144	170	.286	.337	126
Mexico	179	228	.302	.438	163
Argentina	342	433	.503	.639	238
Pakistan	179	211	.170	.200	90

[a] I.e. the manhours required per $ million if prices had been, not at inflated home price levels, but at levels in the Common Market (represented by France). The price indices used were as follows: Spain (114), Brazil (118), Pakistan (118), Argentina (127), Mexico (133). (See Annex Table 11.) Prices in the Common Market were chosen rather than world prices in order to give a fairer comparison.

Source: Calculated on the basis of information available in the Annual Reports of various companies.

Charges Against Capital

We shall define charges against capital (or the gross return on gross assets[8]) as the sum needed to meet depreciation, interest, income and property taxes, and profits. The incidence of these costs will depend upon a) the ratio of assets to output and b) upon the minimum acceptable gross return on assets. As a preliminary working hypothesis, we have assumed that a 15 percent

---

[6] The exception is again Pakistan. As indicated earlier, the Pakistan industry cannot be compared to the heavy industry of Western Europe in the same way as can that of, say, Brazil or Spain. Pakistan produces mainly light and medium transformers and motors with a typically small labor component and a high bought-out component. In this type of production, relatively little supervisory labor is needed.

[7] The figures on which these comparisons were based are shown in Annex Table 10 where they are presented in a somewhat different form.

[8] Defined as gross fixed assets plus gross current assets.

gross return on assets would be acceptable in industrial countries while a 20 percent return would be needed in developing countries.

We have not been able to collect meaningful comparative data on capital costs for specific items of heavy electrical equipment. The difficulties are readily understood when one considers that most heavy items are made to order, and that the average size and type of equipment demanded by the Brazilian electrical power industry differs greatly both from the equipment used in Germany and that used in Mexico.

We made considerable efforts to compare costs in two firms in Spain and Brazil with those in more fully developed countries. We found that gross assets were about 140 percent of sales for the Spanish and the Brazilian firms, whereas in northern Europe they varied from 140 percent (an Austrian firm) to 80 percent (a German and a French firm). These findings suggest that the ratios of assets to sales tend to be lower in fully industrialized countries. However, the difficulties of valuing assets, and incomparability between firms, made this an unreliable measure. Generally, it can be said that the cost of capital for producing a given item of equipment in a developing country is higher a) because the price of the equipment is higher, and so a similar rate of return will indicate a higher capital cost and b) because the rate of return expected in developing countries is also higher. In Table 11 below, we have assumed the real cost is double—though the comparison in the table does not depend on this assumption (see note 9).

Two important operating factors also serve to make capital charges higher in developing countries: the heavy initial operating losses which add greatly

TABLE 11: Cost Structure in the Manufacture of Heavy Electrical Equipment

	Cost W. Europe[a]	Index of Comparative Costs[a]		Cost Developing Countries	
		Spain	Brazil	Spain	Brazil
Materials[b]	51.5	128	133	65.9	68.7
Manpower[c]	35.5	148	126	52.5	44.6
Charges against capital[d]	13.0	200	200	26.0	26.0
	100.0			144.4	139.3
Processing margin[e]	48.5			78.5	70.6

[a] Cost to international manufacturers (in Germany) = 100.
[b] Derived from Table 8.
[c] See Table 10, last column.
[d] Assumed to be double the cost in Western Europe in real terms. See previous section in this chapter.
[e] Margin between selling price and materials costs.

to the cost of the investment; and a low rate of turnover of capital in developing countries compared with the speed with which really efficient producers in industrial countries push a large volume of output through their plants. This also covers the large inventory-carrying cost which mainly arises because of fear of the discontinuity of supply of imported parts and materials.

Combined Impact of Cost Differences

Having considered the three main elements of cost and their variation between industrial and developing countries, we must look into the total impact of observed cost differences. Ideally, we should make this analysis separately for the main classes of equipment: generators, transformers, switchgear, large motors, etc. Since this is impossible for reasons already indicated, we shall start with the cost structure in an industrial country for its entire actual output of heavy electrical equipment and basing ourselves upon our previous analysis of differences in factor costs, ask what this cost structure would look like in a developing country. If that analysis is at all correct, there should be at least a rough order of comparability between the index of comparative cost arrived at in this manner and the comparative prices reviewed in Chapter V. This comparison is shown in Table 11.

According to Table 11, the present product cost disadvantage of Spain and Brazil is of the order of 40 to 45 percent. This difference is greater for Brazil than the difference shown in Annex Table 12. Apart from errors involved in our estimating procedures, one likely explanation is that neither the Brazilian nor the Spanish firm earned anything like the 20 percent gross return on their assets which we have postulated. The paucity of information in official financial statements precludes confirmation of this hypothesis.[9]

The above discussion has been concerned exclusively with comparative *average* costs, making no allowance for the fact that world market prices are based upon marginal costs. According to Annex Table 11, world market prices *c.i.f.* Brazil or Spain would probably be about 10 percent below domestic prices in Western Europe (France). It follows that a price allowing a normal profit margin to producers in Brazil or Spain would be nearly 50 percent higher than the equivalent import price.

Measures of Competitiveness

In the following paragraphs the degree of protection implied in price differences is analyzed by a uniform method. Three different products are used

---

[9] A simple arithmetical example will illustrate the point, however. If actual gross profits in relation to assets were 10 percent only instead of 20 percent, this would reduce the price disadvantage from, say, 40 to 25–30 percent.

66

as examples (Tables 12, 13 and 14). All costs and prices are from the actual operations of the equipment manufacturers. The concepts which we use can be summarized as follows:

α. *Simple Price Difference*—the ratio of domestic price of the product to the *c.i.f.* value of a comparable import. This measure reflects gross protecttion in the price of the final product.

β. *Effective Protection*—the percentage excess of domestic value added over value added in a free trade situation, including freight etc. in value added.[10] It can be measured at each processing stage or at final assembly. In Tables 12, 13 and 14, domestic value added is found by deducting, from the ex-factory price of the Brazilian or Mexican product, all costs of material and service inputs (including depreciation on imported equipment). Value added in a free trade situation is found by obtaining from the manufacturers actual costs for similar material and service inputs in the developed country, and subtracting these from the *c.i.f.* price of the imported product. The difference is "effective protection." It shows the protection enjoyed by the final product compared to the protection enjoyed by its inputs. Effective protection is negative in Tables 12 and 13.

γ. *Domestic resource cost per unit of foreign exchange saved.* This is the domestic resource cost (direct and indirect) of a product over the difference between the *c.i.f.* value of the equipment import and the foreign exchange expenditures (direct and indirect) required for domestic production. It provides a measure of efficiency of the whole industrial sector, including the supplier and sub-supplier industries, for this product. A manufacturing process is not isolated from its environment.

δ. *Adjusted price difference,* the excess (discount) of the price with inputs at international cost levels over the import *c.i.f.* price. This is the protection which the item would require if the domestic manufacturer were to pay for both imported and domestic material inputs, the prices which would have to be paid by an international manufacturer for a like input, given the existing production efficiency. It is lower than the simple price difference by inefficiencies in supplier industries *or* higher-cost material and equipment procurement *or* higher domestic costs caused by protectionism *or* a revenue-oriented customs policy. In the second Brazilian example in Table 13, the measure is negative. This suggests that if inputs could be at international price levels the Brazilian product would be competitive.

---

[10] See Table 12 for definition of value added in this context. Protection is defined as anything which makes it possible for the domestic producer to charge a price higher than the *c.i.f.* price of an *equivalent* import.

TABLE 12: Measurement of Competitiveness, Example 1; Costs and Prices of Manufacture of a Transformer in Brazil against International Prices, 1965

(*million cruzeiros—$Cr 2220 = $US 1*)

		Domestic Manufacture d	International Manufacture[1] i
A. Price　　　　　P		168.8	140.0
B. Directly imported material, cost[2] to plant		61.7	38.1
$\quad$ B$_1$–*f.o.b.* price	44.6		
$\quad$ B$_2$–*c.i.f.* price	48.4		
$\quad$ B$_3$–duty and charges	10.0		
$\quad$ B$_4$–clearing expenses	3.3		
C. Directly imported services[3]		8.4	..
D. Domestic materials[4]		17.9	14.6
$\quad$ D$_1$–import content	2.46		
$\quad$ D$_2$–net of import content	15.48		
E. Other domestic supplies		5.5	4.2
$\quad$ E$_1$–import content	0.8		
$\quad$ E$_2$–net of import content	4.7		
F. Depreciation on imported equipment		3.9	–
G. Foreign exchange expenditure $\quad$ (B$_2$ + C + D$_1$ + E$_1$ + F)		64.0	
H. Materials and services net of import content $\quad$ (D$_2$ + E$_2$)		20.2	
I. Import duty on material (B$_3$)		9.9	
J. Value added (P–B–C–D–E–F)		71.4	83.1
K. Foreign exchange savings $\quad$ (P$_i$ − G)		76.0	
L. Domestic resource cost $\quad$ (P$_d$ − G)		104.8	
α Simple price difference $\quad \dfrac{P_d}{P_i} - 1$		21%	
β Effective protection $\quad \dfrac{J_d}{J_i} - 1$		−14%	
γ Domestic resource cost of unit foreign exchange saved $\quad \dfrac{L}{K} = \dfrac{P_d - G}{P_i - G}$		1.38	
δ Adjusted price difference with inputs at international prices $\dfrac{P_d - (B_d + D_d + E_d) + (B_i + D_i + E_i)}{P_i} - 1$		nil	

Table notes on next page.

[1] Federal Germany. Data are based upon actual costs and prices reported by the manufacturers in the two countries. In international manufacture, they are the actual prices in Germany for the inputs corresponding to those in Brazil (not necessarily the actual cost of inputs in German manufacture). The product price, P_i, is the price *c.i.f.* Brazil, and the value added, J_i, includes in this table the cost of export to Brazil.

[2] Details of imported material landed costs for the Brazilian manufacturer are as follows ($Cr million):

	Inter-national price[a]	*f.o.b.*	*c.i.f.*	Duties & charges	Clearing expenses	Cost to plant
Silicon steel sheets	20.9	22.4[b]	23.9[c]	4.3[d]	1.9[e]	30.1
Copper	11.5[a]	16.0	17.3[f]	–	1.0[g]	18.3
Insulation material	3.6	3.8[h]	4.5[i]	3.6[j]	0.2[k]	8.3
Bushings (high tension)	2.1	2.4[l]	2.7[m]	2.1[n]	0.2[o]	5.0
Total	38.1	44.6	48.4	10.0	3.3	61.7

[a] *f.a.s.* except for copper, which is based on the London Metal Exchange price, whereas the international price is based on the producer price.

[b] Export expenses 7 percent *f.a.s.*

[c] Freight 5.9 percent *f.o.b.*, insurance 0.6 percent *f.o.b.*

[d] Import duties and charges 18 percent *c.i.f.*

[e] Clearing expenses 6.75 percent of duty-paid cost.

[f] Freight 2.3 percent *f.o.b.* and insurance 0.2 percent *f.o.b.*, banking expenses 5.6 percent *f.o.b.*

[g] No duty on copper import, only customs expenses of 6 percent *f.o.b.*

[h] Export charges 6.7 percent *f.a.s.*

[i] Freight 10.7 percent *f.a.s.*, insurance 0.9 percent *f.a.s.*, banking expenses 6.1 percent *f.a.s.*

[j] Customs duty and charges 80 percent *c.i.f.*

[k] Clearing expenses 4.5 percent of *c.i.f.* value.

[l] Export expenses 15 percent *f.a.s.*

[m] Freight 5.6 percent *f.o.b.*, insurance 1 percent *f.o.b.*, banking expenses 5.8 percent *f.o.b.*

[n] Duties 76 percent *c.i.f.*

[o] Customs expenses 7.5 percent *c.i.f.*

Note: Amounts may not be exact owing to rounding.

[3] Engineering charges for the whole plant were 11 percent of the total sales, of which 5 percent were foreign and 6 percent local engineering.

[4] Details of domestic material costs are as follows: ($Cr million)

	Value	Import content (percent)	Value net of import	Value of import content
Steel plates	3.44	8	3.16	0.28
Parts and components	14.50	15	12.32	2.18
	17.94		15.48	2.46

TABLE 13: Measurement of Competitiveness, Example 2: Cost and Price of Manufacture of a Generator in Brazil against International Prices, 1965

(U.S. $)

	Domestic Manufacture d	International Manufacture i
A. Price P	20,800[a]	19,600
B. Directly imported material, cost to plant	3,370[b]	1,980
B_1–f.o.b. 2,703		
B_2–c.i.f. 2,795		
B_3–duty 575		
C. Directly imported services	321	..
D. Domestic material	5,309[c]	3,795
D_1–import content 1,539		
D_2–net of import content 3,770		
E. Other domestic supplies	1,800	1,380
E_1–import content 200		
E_2–net of import content 1,600		
F. Depreciation on imported equipment	160	–
G. Foreign exchange expenditure $(B_2 + C + D_1 + E_1 + F)$	5,015	
H. Materials and services net of import content $(D_2 + E_2)$	5,370	
I. Import duty on material (B_3)	575	
J. Value added (P–B–C–D–E–F)	9,840	12,445
K. Foreign exchange savings $P_i - G$	14,585	
L. Domestic resource cost $P_d - G$	15,785	
α Simple price difference $\dfrac{P_d}{P_i} - 1$	6%	
β Effective protection $\dfrac{J_d}{J_i} - 1$	−20.9%	
γ Domestic resource cost of unit foreign exchange saved (L/K) $\dfrac{P_d - G}{P_i - G}$	1.08	
δ Adjusted price difference with inputs at international prices $\dfrac{P_d - (B_d + D_d + E_d) + (B_i + D_i + E_i)}{P_i} - 1$	−11%	

[a] The list price of this product was about US $33,000 in the industrial country, Federal Germany. With the maximum reduction available (31.0 percent) at the time of reporting, the normal purchase price in the international market was about US $22,800. But because of special trade agreements, mainly with Eastern bloc countries, the price of imported equip-

70

Table 12 shows the calculation of these concepts for one product in Brazil, expressed in local currency. Once the rate of exchange (or conversion) is decided upon, all values, whether domestic or foreign, can be expressed in local currencies. The same calculation can be carried out in foreign currency, for instance, in US dollars. Table 13 shows such a calculation for another product in Brazil. In fact, we can express all values in percent of a base, for instance, of the international price. The computation then becomes simpler and the presentation more compact—see Table 14, which shows the calculation for a product in Mexico.

In order to calculate effective protection or domestic resource cost per unit of foreign exchange saved, a detailed cost breakdown of individual products is required. Even if one has detailed information on the cost of each product it is still difficult, if not impossible, to aggregate the results and arrive at "one" figure for the protection of the industry unless the industry produces only a single product. In heavy electrical equipment, due to the differences in product type—sizes as well as domestic content—the cost structure cannot be easily generalized. The price also varies from product to product. Thus using one or two products as representative of the industry may be misleading.

---

ment in developing countries was US $19,600. Thus local manufacturers and other exporters had to reduce their prices close to that level. Since our calculation (cost structure) is based on actual figures we preferred to use the prices prevailing at that time.

b The breakdown of the directly imported material costs for Brazil are as follows (US $/ton):

| | International Manufacture at Plant | Domestic Manufacture | | | |
		f.o.b.	c.i.f.	Charges on import	At plant
Silicone steel	440	453	505	295	800
Copper (insulated)	1,540	2,250	2,290	280	2,570
Total	1,980	2,703	2,795	575	3,370

Note: Since the data were collected during the copper crisis, the price for copper in developing countries differs greatly from the producers' price.

c The components of domestic material costs are as follows (US dollars):

| | For International Manufacturer | For Domestic Manufacturer | | | |
	Purchase price	Purchase price	Net of import	Import content (percent)	Import content value
Carbon steel	590	672	619	8	53
Insulation	225	407	326	20	81
Tooling	1,800	2,700	1,754	35	946
Parts and others	1,180	1,530	1,071	30	459
Total	3,795	5,309	3,770		1,539

71

TABLE 14: Measurement of Competitiveness, Example 3: Cost and Price of Manufacture of a Capacitor in Mexico against International Prices, 1965[a]

(quoted price of international manufacturer = 100)

	Manufacturer in Mexico d	International Manufacturer i	Percentage Difference	
Price	155.00	100.0	+55	*Simple price difference*
Material and auxiliary inputs	80.68	55.38	+46	*Protection on inputs*
Material	74.89	51.50	+45	*Protection on material inputs*
Imported, cost to plant	34.89	26.00	+34	*Protection with respect to imported material (customs duties and freight)*
F.o.b.	27.60			
C.i.f.	31.48			
Duties	3.41			
Locally procured material	40.00	25.50	+57	*Protection on supply industries (with some imported inputs)*
Indirect import content	7.00			
Net of import content	33.00		+78[b]	*Protection on supply industries, net of import content*
Services and production supplies	5.79	3.88	+49	*Protection on services & production supplies*
Services	4.81	3.33[c]		
Electricity	0.46	0.55		
Insurance	0.39	0.26		
Rent	3.84	2.40		
Freight	0.12	0.12		
Production Supplies	0.98	0.55[c]		
Fuels and lubricants	0.46	0.23		

Indirect material		0.12	0.11	
Tools		0.40	0.21	
Import content of services and supplies		0.41	—	
Depreciation				
On imported equipment		1.60	1.60	
On building and locally procured equipment		1.90	—	
Royalties and license fees		4.42		
Value added		68.30	44.62	+53 *Effective protection*
Foreign exchange expenditure		44.91		
Direct	35.90			
Indirect	7.41			
Depreciation	1.60			
Foreign exchange saved		55.09		
Domestic resource cost		110.09		+2.0 *Domestic resource cost per unit of foreign exchange saved (ratio)*
Domestic prices with inputs at international prices		129.70	100.0	+30 *Adjusted price difference*[d]

a Cost figures are based on actual costs paid by two corresponding companies unless otherwise indicated. Prices are taken from an international competition in which both firms participated.
b This is arrived at as follows: 33 ÷ (25.50 − 7.00) = 1.78.
c These are estimated on the basis of general information given in the industrial census of the developed country.

d Considering only the material inputs:
$$\delta = \frac{155.00 - 74.89 + 51.50}{100} = \frac{131.61}{100}$$
Thus adjusted price difference would be 31.6 percent.

Table 15 shows the effects of differences in domestic content and prices, derived from direct information on 12 different products. In order to simplify the calculation it is assumed that there is no foreign exchange cost for know-how and similar services, or for maintenance (depreciation). These are relatively small costs in our examples (see items C and F in Tables 12 and 13). In effect this means that they are included as value added. It is further assumed that the price differential between domestically supplied materials and material inputs for manufacture in a free trade situation is equal to the tariff and other charges (e.g. profits of importers if any) on directly imported material. Thus only one price differential P_r is calculated for all material and supplies. If one is interested in a more elaborate calculation, one must assign international prices to each input of the industry, and add them. The main conclusion one can draw from the widely differing results for separate products in Table 15, perhaps, is how dangerous it is to make generalizations about a country's industrial competitiveness.

Full discussion of the merits of the concepts of effective protection and domestic resource cost of foreign exchange savings would be beyond the scope of the present study. The aim here is to form an idea about the performance of the industry under a given set of conditions, at a given moment of time. Such a picture is certainly static in nature and does not reflect the dynamics of the industry. It is only true under a given set of conditions, in international as well as internal markets for products and inputs. However, to form a quantitative dynamic picture is formally difficult, and here in fact impossible, because of the lack of historical data about costs. In the next section we will discuss the domestic resource cost of foreign exchange savings for one year, 1964, and comment qualitatively on the dynamics of manufacturing costs in the following chapter.

Foreign Exchange Savings

The heavy electrical equipment industry in the developing countries has been established for import substitution. We could not identify any plant built to produce for export or to serve a regional market.[11]

Foreign exchange savings may be expressed as the difference between two magnitudes:

a) the foreign exchange component (materials, services, license fees, etc.) of the domestic product, and

---

[11] Several entrepreneurs who selected Brazil or Argentina have had the potential market of LAFTA in mind, but no existing entrepreneur appears to have entered the industry with export intentions.

TABLE 15: Protection and Domestic Resource Cost per Unit of Foreign Exchange Saved for 12 Individual Products

| | Material Inputs as percent of Domestic Final Product[a] | | Price Indices | | Simple Price Difference (*percent*) α | Effective Protection (*percent*) β | Domestic Resource Cost per Unit of Foreign Exchange Saved γ | Price Difference with Material Inputs at International Costs (*percent*) δ |
	Domestic d	Imported m	Import *c.i.f.* price = 1 P_d	International cost of material inputs = 1 P_r				
Brazil:								
Product 1:	30	12	1.20	1.54	20	3	1.23	2
2:	12	34	1.46	1.15	46	90	1.92	37
3:	12	6	1.50	1.34	50	54	1.57	43
4:	26	24	1.06	1.46	6	−17	1.08	−11
Mexico:								
Product 1:	40	40	1.20	1.35	20	−17	1.39	−5
2:	34	45	.90	1.32	−10	−59	0.83	−27
3:	26	45	1.40	1.33	40	60	2.08	15
4:	22	55	1.28	1.32	28	16	1.96	4
5:	22	23	1.67	1.31	67	115	2.08	49
Pakistan:								
Product 1:	23	42	1.71	1.61	71	93	3.53	28
2:	27	30	1.49	1.67	49	30	1.89	15
3:	22	32	1.78	1.44	78	147	2.83	48

[a] Including production supplies, e.g. electricity, fuel, etc.

Note: $\alpha = (P_d - 1) \times 100;$

$$\beta = \left(\frac{1-(d+m)}{\frac{1}{P_d} - \frac{d+m}{P_r}} - 1 \right) \times 100;$$

$$\gamma = \frac{1-m}{\frac{1}{P_d} - m};$$

$$\delta = \left(P_d \left(1 - (d+m) + \frac{d+m}{P_r} \right) - 1 \right) \times 100.$$

75

b) the foreign exchange cost of the imported product it replaces.

But foreign exchange saving is not an end in itself. To calculate its economic benefits, we must relate this saving to the effort expended in achieving it. More precisely, we must look at the ratio between the production cost expenditure in local currency and the net foreign exchange savings measured in dollars. This is then compared with the actual exchange rate.[12] Such calculations have been made in Table 16 (p. 78). The figures cannot be used to judge the relative performance of individual countries (or their long-run competitive advantage) since these countries are at different stages of learning. Nevertheless, they give a rough idea of their performances in 1964.

The figures in Table 16 should be interpreted with caution, and represent no more than preliminary indications of a country's position at a certain point of time. They depend on the estimates of:

a) the average difference between the world market price level for heavy electrical equipment and the country's price levels;
b) the import component in the total selling price; and
c) the exchange rate used.

We have refrained from entering into methodological discussion. Theoretical considerations have been well described elsewhere. In the end, one is always faced with a choice between what is practically attainable and significant and what might be theoretically desirable. Three issues illustrate this point:

a) It has been argued that one should exclude indirect taxes from domestic costs. But taxes are part of the cost structure and have to be paid one way or another. In some countries, taxes cover services which in other countries would be reflected in social security charges (which are a labor cost) or would be paid by wage and salary earners themselves (*ceteris paribus,* higher wages).

b) According to the method used here, an industry is "penalized" (gets a low comparative advantage ratio) independently of whether the main disadvantage lies in supplier industries or in the subsequent manufacture of equipment based upon purchased materials and components. It would be of some interest to recalculate what the comparative advantage figures would be on the assumption that all materials and purchased components could be obtained at world market prices, including freight, transport, etc. But even for relatively standard items it is not easy to compute what these market prices

---

[12] See M. Bruno, *Interdependence, Resource Use and Structural Change in Israel,* Bank of Israel, Jerusalem, 1962.

would be (considering volume of purchase, quality, payment conditions), and there are many materials (e.g. castings, forgings, etc.) and purchased components for which there are no published market prices. Hence, we have preferred to focus here on the *actual* cost of the *total* domestic component.

c) In principle, we should take account of the foreign exchange component of domestic inputs in addition to direct imports. The indirect import component is included here only where some major semi-manufactures (e.g. of copper and brass) having a large import content are purchased on the domestic market. Since seven or eight major materials cover 90 to 95 percent of the total materials consumed, it is unlikely that major indirect inputs have been overlooked. Certain inputs, e.g. paint, probably have an import content but their share in the total cost in negligible.

It should also be noted that, in some cases, the domestic cost includes an element of protective duty on materials. This would tend to somewhat overstate comparative disadvantage; on balance, we feel this bias is not too important.

Review of Findings

The preceding discussions may be broadly summarized as follows:

a) Domestic prices exceed import prices by 25 to 30 percent in Spain and Brazil. The difference is slightly higher in Argentina and Mexico—40 to 45 percent.

b) The ratios between the electrical equipment "shadow" exchange rates and the actual exchange rates for Spain, Brazil and Argentina are in the range of 1.5 to 1.75.[13]

c) The economic results are worse in Mexico, with a similar domestic content but rather higher prices, particularly for electric motors. They are especially poor in Pakistan, where a moderate price difference is associated with a low domestic component.

However, substantively, the above comparisons do not indicate the extent to which high prices may be due to a) the industry still being in an infant stage; b) though past the infant stage, suffering from disabilities which could at least in theory be repaired, like poor industry structure, poor management, or monopoly pricing; or c) certain more permanent disabilities such as a low volume of output or relatively high costs for certain production factors.

---

[13] In all these countries, the domestic component is approximately 50 percent, so that a 25 to 30 percent price difference would normally imply a 50 to 60 percent effective protection.

TABLE 16: Measuring the Foreign Exchange Savings of the Industry, Six Countries, 1964

	Spain	Brazil	Argen-tina	Mexico	India	Pakis-tan	formula
1. Output of sample firms[a] (*millions of domestic currency*)	1,500	21,500	1,652	212.5	45	42.8	—
2. Relevant exchange rate[b] US $1 =	60	1,505	262	12.5	4.75	4.75	—
3. Output, value in US dollars (*$ millions*)	25	14.3	6.3	17.0	9.5	9.0	P_d
4. Imports of materials, components, etc. (*$ millions*)							—
5. License fees, know-how payments (*$ millions*)		4.2		5.2	3.3	5.4	—
6. Depreciation on imported equipment (*$ millions*)		0.6		0.7	0.8	0.2	
		0.5		0.7	2.7	0.2	
7. Imported inputs, total (*$ millions*)[c]	10	5.3	2.2	6.6	6.8	5.8	m
8. Index of comparative price level[d]	1.25	1.30	1.40	1.45	1.60	1.30	$\dfrac{P_d}{P_i}$
9. Import component in domestic price (line 7 ÷ line 3)	0.40	0.37	0.35	0.40	0.72	0.65	$\dfrac{m}{P_d}$
10. Foreign exchange savings as ratio of import price[e] (1 − line 8 × line 9)	0.50	0.52	0.51	0.42	−0.15	0.16	$1 - \dfrac{m}{P_i}$
11. Present competitiveness $\dfrac{\text{(line 3 − line 7)}}{\text{(line 3 ÷ line 8 − line 7)}}$	1.50	1.59	1.77	2.02	(−)	2.76	$\dfrac{P_d - m}{P_i - m}$

price are shown in some detail for countries other than Spain and Argentina. The figures for Spain and Argentina are very rough estimates.

[d] Taking the equivalent world market *c.i.f.* import price P_i as 100 in each case. Details for individual countries are shown below:

Spain: Based upon estimates provided by international manufacturers with experience regarding the Spanish market and in interviews with Spanish manufacturers.

Brazil: Based upon estimated price differences of 50 percent for generators, 35 percent for transformers and 25 percent for heavy motors, each group weighted according to the value of domestic output. (Generators have a comparatively small weighting.)

Argentina: The index used for Argentina may be on the low side. Figures for four selected items (2,100 kva generator, 0.5, 20, and 40 Mva transformers, indicate a range of price differences of 38–69 percent, with an unweighted average of 51 percent.

Mexico: Giving equal weight (total sales volume) to motors and transformers, and assuming a price index of 1.15 for transformers and 1.75 for motors, we arrive at an over-all index of 145.

India: Figure quoted by a foreign expert who has been following Bhopal progress closely.

Pakistan: Using price indices of 1.2 for transformers, 1.35 for switchgear and 1.42 for electric motors. Transformers represent about 44 percent of the sales volume, motors 31 percent, and switchgear 25 percent.

[e] This figure which is mentioned in the text is the most immediate indicator of direct foreign exchange savings.

[a] The output covered in 1964 was estimated as follows:

Spain: Very rough estimate (based on published statistics and interviews) of domestic output of generators, transformers above 1,000 kva, heavy motors (above 100 hp), traction equipment, high-tension switchgear, etc.

Brazil: Combined output of two largest firms.

Argentina: Very crude approximation based upon incomplete data submitted by four leading firms.

Mexico: Combined output of transformers, motors, and accessories, including small motors.

India: Heavy Electricals (India) Ltd.; Eighth Annual Report covering the year ended March 31, 1964.

Pakistan: Estimated domestic production of transformers, motors, and switchgear of all sizes.

[b] The Argentine exchange rate was derived from the adjusted exchange rate for December 1965 (see Annex A) by dividing this adjusted rate by the index of wholesale prices for December 1965 (1964 = 100). The Brazilian rate was based on the free rate established in November 1965 of Cr. $2,220 per US $1, or Cr. $2,470, allowing for certain surcharges and compulsory deposits. It was assumed that this rate was an "equilibrium rate." A corresponding rate for 1964 was derived by dividing the November 1965 rate by the wholesale price index for the same month (1964 = 100). For all other countries, the rates used were the official exchange rates. In view of the subsequent devaluation, the procedure probably gives too high an exchange value for the Indian currency, thus understating India's comparative advantage.

[c] The major imported inputs as a proportion of the selling

VII

THE DYNAMICS OF COMPETITIVENESS

In earlier discussions we have been concerned only with a comparison of *actual* costs and prices. We must now consider how these costs are influenced by market size, the "learning process," and the institutional framework. Thus some elements of a dynamic nature are introduced.

Market

Figure 9 gives a rough picture of the 1964 relationship between per capita income and per capita spending on heavy electrical equipment (including steam turbines and related equipment). Total spending on heavy electrical equipment in 1964 was of the order shown below:

Sweden	$190 million
Switzerland, Spain, India	$130 to 135 million
Mexico	$120 million
Austria, Brazil	$ 75 to 100 million

The European countries are important exporters of heavy electrical equipment, mainly to other European countries, and (this seems crucially important) their imports are as large as their exports. The presumption is that

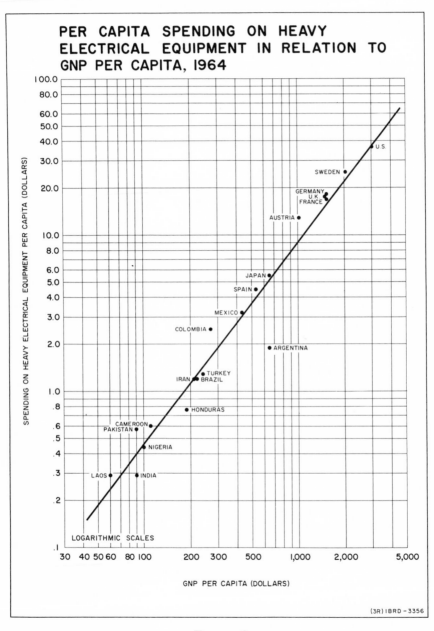

PER CAPITA SPENDING ON HEAVY ELECTRICAL EQUIPMENT IN RELATION TO GNP PER CAPITA, 1964

FIGURE 9

81

the market in Sweden would not be large enough to permit reasonable economies of scale and specialization but for the fact that one-third of the total output is exported. Similarly the Austrian market would not be nearly large enough but for the fact that two-thirds of the total output is exported. The main products are equipment for the generation and transmission of power. The demand for heavy electrical equipment for industrial uses and traction probably follows a roughly similar pattern, with great variations for individual countries. Diesel-electric locomotives are made in both India and Sweden on US licenses. In Sweden, the electrical component, representing about one-third of the total cost, is imported; in India, it is manufactured locally. Differences in market size and in the policies of the licensors may be part of the explanation. But it may also reflect different national policies—one based upon trade and comparative advantage, the other one on self-sufficiency and industrialization, irrespective of comparative advantage. Finally, all three European countries (Sweden, Austria and Switzerland) produce hydroelectrical equipment, mainly needed in their domestic markets.

Recognizing the apparent existence of economies of scale in the manufacture of heavy electrical equipment, the next problem is to identify them. Only some tentative guesses are ventured in this area. The most obvious advantages of scale are in research and development. If a company delivers, say, five 500,000 kva generators per year, rather than one such generator every other year, its chances of writing off development expense are immensely increased. It is not entirely clear how much effort it takes for a subsidiary of an international concern, say in Brazil, to absorb experience gained by its parent in Switzerland or in the United States in making a new-size generator. If the transfer of such experience is very efficient, there will be only moderate scale economies on this score.

Compared to the technology of generators or switchgear, that of transformer manufacture is simple and the number of units purchased is larger (particularly for intermediate systems transformers and distribution transformers). Even so, a large industrial country such as the United Kingdom needs only about 500 systems transformers per year. Though flow line techniques have been developed for assembling such transformers, the massive operations of winding and testing generally have to be carried out separately.[1] On balance, therefore, economies of scale in transformer manufacture are probably modest, and would not normally preclude their manufacture in fair-sized industrializing countries, as long as a certain minimum demand can be foreseen over a period of years, for a given type and size class.

---

[1] See "Transforming Transformers," *The Economist*, May 20, 1967, p. 822.

In manufacturing generators, it would seem that the principal factor in realizing scale economies is *enough work spread uniformly* so as to keep existing producers busy. Roughly speaking, this requirement is likely to be met by one order for a large generator every 18 months. Costs could be reduced if major power supply companies established long-term plans, giving the estimated composition of their future equipment demand. In the United Kingdom, the Central Electricity Generating Board makes a ten-year projection of its switchgear requirements which has been followed up, at regular intervals, with "bulk allocation" of work between the (then) four manufacturers. The first step permits the manufacturers to make long-run investment in production facilities; the second step enables them to go ahead with production planning and supplier contracts.[2, 3]

Such allocation of contracts should not, however, conflict with competitive bidding. Any departures from this principle, such as direct negotiation or restricted bidding, should be only such as will push domestic producers towards competitive international standards, or force a streamlining of the industry structure if there are too many producers.

As already indicated, the whole European heavy electrical equipment industry is undergoing concentration. It seems highly likely that there are also too many producers of hydraulic generators in Brazil (2), or of medium switchgear in Argentina (3), or, taking an illustration from light equipment, of distribution transformers and electric motors in India (17 and 25 respectively of some importance, plus a large number of very small manufacturers).[4] Governments have sometimes justified their encouragement or toleration of an excessive number of producers by alleging the benefits of competition. But protected competition in a small pond may lead to an excessive number of weak fish. Within the LAFTA area, economic production of heavy electrical

---

[2] See G. B. Richardson, "The Pricing of Heavy Electrical Equipment: Competition or Agreement," *Oxford University Bulletin of Economics and Statistics*, May 1966, p. 86. The problem of feeding orders to as many as four suppliers was one of the factors which led the authorities to support mergers between manufacturers. In most sectors of heavy electrical industry, there are now only two competitors.

[3] The importance of careful market study for economic production can hardly be overstated. Such studies, according to experts, should cover at least a 15-year span, and should project the breakdown between hydro and thermal capacity, the length and voltage of transmission lines, the size of generators and transformers, the demand for heavy electrical equipment by manufacturing industries and railroads, etc. Some of the plants visited embarked upon manufacture without clearly identifying the future structure of demand and later were forced to diversify operations in order to fill unused capacity, sometimes duplicating lines of established producers, even outside the electrical equipment field.

[4] For details, see Annex Table 14. In South Africa, there are five manufacturers of motors up to 250 hp. We are told that, with standardization, one would be sufficient.

equipment might be possible, but probably only with a limited number of producers, orderly procurement by power companies, free trade within the area and, at least in the beginning, moderate protection against imports from the outside.[5] If equipment manufacturers have merged their operations in Western Europe (though not yet over national boundaries), corporate policies may conceivably not be an absolute obstacle to mergers overseas.

Learning Process

In arriving at competitive manufacture of heavy electrical equipment in developing countries, it is convenient perhaps to distinguish three steps of the learning process:

a) initial learning
b) gradual buildup of capability
c) independent research and development potential.

In the first step, skilled labor has to be recruited and trained, supply capabilities developed, expatriate managerial personnel adjusted to decision-making in an entirely new environment, and a flow of orders secured in the face of buyer skepticism regarding product quality and on-time delivery. In one case, a well-known heavy electrical firm invested as much money in training programs and early operating losses in its overseas subsidiary as its whole fixed plant investment. There is a dilemma here. If one wants to compress the period for achieving optimum plant operation, one has to recruit on a large scale for multiple-shift operation, and the investment in manpower goes up. If, on the other hand, one follows a more gradual course, plant utilization stays low and long delivery times may make the firm less competitive. If on top of this, the infant industry fails to secure an adequate volume of orders (because of irregular procurement, poor market research, exchange rate overvaluation, etc.) it will be in deep trouble. Annex B gives some actual productivity profiles for the learning period but these are too fragmentary and the difficulties in year-to-year comparisons are too great

---

[5] At the third sectoral meeting of Latin American manufacturers of generators, transmission and distribution equipment (May 21 to 31, 1967), the delegations represented agreed to present a joint recommendation to the international financial organizations suggesting that the benefits (preferences) which are accorded to national manufacturers should be extended to the manufacturers in other member countries. For their part the delegations from Brazil and Mexico concluded a project for a "complementation agreement," according to which all duties and restrictions would be removed in the trade between the two countries in a number of products. They agreed to ask their respective governments for official formulation of the agreement.

to permit safe generalizations. Under favorable circumstances, the learning period for heavy electrical equipment production with well established technology in an industrial though still developing environment can probably be reduced to four or five years. In actual fact, it is perhaps likely to reach seven years or even more, if the environment is unsuitable or if there are unforeseen difficulties.

The problem of growth in capabilities was discussed previously in Chapter IV. Because of the trend towards large units, any new manufacturer of heavy electrical equipment has a strong incentive to strive towards new frontiers of production experience. It is doubtful whether this can be achieved economically through license agreements. It is certainly achieved more easily by a local affiliate of an international concern. In the latter case, the main cost is in the initial learning period. Growth into new capabilities becomes a natural process, less burdensome to the developing country than the similar phase some years earlier in the industrial country.

Even major technical advances are readily introduced where the domestic producer has strong corporate ties with a large international concern. Where this knowledge has to be acquired by an independent producer through license or know-how agreements, on the other hand, there is a danger that he may stay too long with the originally acquired technology. Often he would lack an independent technical capability permitting him to adjust promptly to new techniques or changes in the relative prices of major inputs (say aluminum versus copper). To establish such a capability in an early stage of industrialization is probably not economical. First, the advantages of scale in research and development are one major reason for recent and proposed mergers in Western Europe. Secondly, developing countries have no comparative advantage in this area: salaries of research personnel are high, and the research environment is more difficult.

If our observations on the learning process are correct, they would suggest the following pattern of infant industry protection:

a) An initial period of protection could be provided each time a new major line of manufacture is taken up. This would last, say, seven years.

b) The actual rate of protection could be based upon a realistic appraisal of the average cost difference between domestic and imported equipment during the infant period. The exact level of protection might be a matter for negotiation between the government and the interested producers. The main end sought by the government is presumably competitiveness at the end of the learning period. Within this framework, a production license might be given to that manufacturer or manufacturing group which, under otherwise equal conditions, would be satisfied with the smallest protection.

When comparing costs and prices, we defined the institutional framework as *those conditions, including in particular government policies, which would make actual costs exceed costs determined by the country's comparative advantage.* Though appropriate to the discussion of comparative costs, this definition should be elaborated for more general analysis. It views the institutional framework as a negative factor. It may be said with equal justice, however, that the institutional framework "encompasses those instruments which enable a country to realize its full industrial potential." In brief, the institutional framework may support or thwart healthy growth.

The emphasis is on the word "healthy." Historically, the manufacture of heavy electrical equipment in the countries studied was started in response to the twin desires of governments to industrialize and of the international manufacturers of heavy electrical equipment to preserve and expand markets. To this end, governments were normally prepared to provide heavy protection and sometimes additional incentives. Protection[6] was clearly the indispensable condition for the establishment of the industry since, in all cases, heavy electrical equipment could be imported from abroad at prices lower than those of the prospective domestic producers.

Yet, even if we accept protection as a necessary condition, certain policies adopted under this umbrella will have a major bearing upon production costs. These policies may be considered under four headings:

Shape of protection. Protection should be time-limited and held as low as possible, recognizing that excessive protection breeds inefficiency and is inextricably interwoven with, and tends to perpetuate, economic controls and poor industrial structure. Protection should not become a compensation for inefficient management or for bad planning. It is only justified for industries which are economically viable in the country concerned and efficiently managed. In this case the industry will presumably become internationally competitive as soon as the difficulties of the learning stage are passed.

Number of producers. An excessive number of producers is likely to result from excessive initial protection. This type of industrial structure should be discouraged. Mergers across national frontiers in the same geographic area should be promoted.

Economic controls. Economic controls, to a large extent, are a by-product

---

[6] We define protection as *any measure taken by the government which makes it possible for the domestic producer to charge a price higher than the c.i.f. price of equivalent imports.*

of foreign exchange stringencies. We are not concerned here, however, with possible justification but only with visible effects. Some manufacturers of heavy electrical equipment were not granted sufficient foreign exchange to complete their plants; delays resulted. Many plants encountered a more acute difficulty: after only a few months of operation, they suffered import restrictions on needed materials and components. This caused high costs because of unused capacity and idle trained personnel. Yet the worst damage is probably an environmental one: management is diverted away from productive tasks or left idle.

Procurement. Procurement should be based upon a long-range plan, taking into account the need for competitiveness and for sound utilization of existing capacity.

Besides protection, the major factor affecting the development of heavy electrical equipment production has been the climate for foreign investment. In developing countries it has been virtually impossible to manufacture heavy electrical equipment economically without the support of international manufacturers; it should normally be advantageous for government policy to smooth the path for such participation. The lines of the general policies to promote international investment (e.g. political stability, guaranteed transfer of earnings, reasonable protection against expropriation, satisfactory labor relations) are well known.

Something should be said, however, about economic nationalism. This word is used here in a purely descriptive sense, concerned only with proximate economic effects. (No attempt is made here to evaluate or to judge political necessities or psychological or emotional factors.) Economic nationalism has many facets, e.g. insistence upon:

a) minimum domestic shareholdings or even the acceptance of specified domestic partners;

b) limitations upon the employment of foreign technicians; or

c) limitations upon license fees.

Some policy moves in these directions have in practice often turned out to be self-defeating. Many foreign companies are anxious to find domestic partners and/or sell shares locally. An unsuitable domestic partner forced upon a sound international producer reduces the attractiveness of the investment. Similarly, many foreign companies in this industry are anxious to replace their own nationals with local personnel; France, Germany, Sweden, Switzerland are all short of key staff, and very great capability is required to succeed in a developing country. Limitations on license fees, in a competitive situation, may merely impose similar needless obstacles.

VIII

SUMMARY AND CONCLUSIONS

Characteristics of the Industry

The heavy electrical equipment industry, in the definition we have adopted, covers the production of power generating and transmission equipment together with certain industrial items such as heavy traction equipment and electric furnaces.

Such equipment is generally custom-designed and much of it is large and expensive. It therefore calls for design capability and substantial skill and care at the manufacturing end. Large investments are required in testing facilities and, increasingly, in heavy handling and machining facilities.

To keep plant and skilled manpower occupied becomes a prime objective for management. This is made difficult by the fact that orders are typically very large, few and infrequent. One order or one piece of equipment may absorb 10 to 20 percent of the annual production capacity of even a relatively large heavy electrical equipment firm, and the trend is towards even larger units. Hence, if there are three manufacturers of turbines or generators for hydropower applications, only one may receive an order in a given year; even if there is only one manufacturer he may have no orders for this type of equipment in years when expansion is focused on thermal generating capacity. This situation, one suspects, is one reason why most major companies have tried to produce a full line of heavy electrical equipment which, in turn, forces

88

them to keep in touch with a large number of technologies and manufacturing techniques.

The industry is very dependent upon outside financing. Fixed investments are perhaps not unusually high but much capital is tied up in inventories and work-in-progress. At the same time, at least in developing countries, the customers want credit; some of the equipment (e.g. hydro) they purchase will last 30 to 50 years and upwards, and their receipts from the output of this equipment will come in only slowly.

International Structure

The total annual demand for heavy electrical equipment (outside Comecon countries) is estimated at US $16 billion, of which 80 percent comes from ten industrialized countries. Trade is important, even among the major producing countries, but is largely restricted to items not produced in the importing country. World exports are valued at $2.2 billion equivalent; of these $0.9 billion go to industrialized countries and $1.1 billion to developing countries. Some medium-sized industrialized countries like Sweden, Belgium and Austria are virtually self-sufficient on a net basis; yet their imports of heavy electrical equipment range from 40 to 60 percent of their total consumption. The developing countries are large importers. As a group, they account for the major portion of world imports of hydraulic generating equipment, transformers and switchgear.

The industry is dominated by a limited number of large companies, practically all of which are engaged in international operations. Many of the international firms produce both heavy and light electrical equipment and the largest ones have branched out substantially into related fields. Nevertheless, several major producers have heavy electrical equipment as their main production line. Major firms like General Electric, Siemens and Brown Boveri have manufacturing interests in a number of industrialized countries as well as in several of the developing countries studied.

Because of intensive competition in conventional items of equipment, the bulk of the profits are earned on items where a particular firm has pioneered new developments. Investments in research and development are enormous.

A pronounced trend towards very large individual units of generators and transformers has created excess capacity, since it takes far fewer man-hours and machine time to produce one large generator than to produce two small generators of the same combined rating. Excess capacity combined with the large capital requirements for research and development (and increasing competition within the Common Market) have led to a wave of mergers in Western Europe.

Excess capacity also explains the jealous protection of national markets and

89

the attempts to extend these markets abroad through various financial and other arrangements, particularly tied aid. Finally, it lies behind the very sharp price competition on the free world market and has encouraged attempts to get around this by direct manufacturing investments in protected markets abroad.

The Industry in Developing Countries

We have analyzed the experience of six countries—Spain, Brazil, Argentina, Mexico, India and Pakistan. In *Spain*, the manufacture of heavy electrical equipment on a substantial scale dates from World War II. There has been gradual and efficient growth during the post-war period. Spain leads the other developing countries in capabilities, has the lowest prices, and has developed some exports. Nevertheless, the industry is not as yet price-competitive in the world market. The future shift in Spain from hydro-power to large thermal (mainly nuclear) power stations is probably the major difficulty and the major challenge faced by the Spanish industry today.

The most impressive growth has been in *Brazil*. Since 1958, it has been moving towards self-reliance with a very rapid buildup of capabilities. Enormous efforts have been made, particularly by two large international companies, in creating modern facilities to produce very large equipment, in recruiting and training manpower, in developing supplier potentials, and in gaining production experience. Though there have been great strides in competitiveness, prices are still rather high, profitability poor, and capacity in excess of needs.

Until now, the production of heavy electrical equipment in *Mexico* and *Argentina* has been limited mainly to transformers and motors, with some small generators being built in Argentina. In Mexico, one firm dominates the industry and has apparently achieved good results in transformer production. In contrast, prices for motors are high—the market may not permit reasonable economies of scale. In Argentina, there are two major producers of power transformers and switchgear. The industry has been troubled by excessive product diversification and unused capacity.

In *India*, the private sector manufacturing transformers and motors grew rapidly in 1950–1963. There are many firms, all small by international standards. Prices are quite low, but the industry has lagged behind in technology. This may be due, in part, to rigidities caused by economic controls. The Indian Government entered into the production of generators, turbines, and heavy switchgear through public enterprises, and construction was begun at Bhopal, in 1958, of a large plant to manufacture most of these items. Subsequently, three more specialized plants have been built at other locations. The total investment in Bhopal at the end of March 1965 was about $125 million equivalent, including accumulated losses. Sales were about 15 percent of the planned output. The recession of 1966 and 1967 did not advance the industry's profitability. Clearly, Bhopal experienced enormous difficulties, one of which was perhaps trying to do too many things too fast.

Pakistan's production of electrical equipment for power system and industrial uses does not, as yet, include much heavy equipment. In the early 1960's manufacture of transformers, motors and switchgear was strongly promoted by the government, and, in 1965, domestic producers (all private) supplied more than one-half of the total demand for electric motors and transformers. Prices are still high by international standards.

Price Comparisons

World market prices for heavy electrical equipment have fallen sharply in recent years, and there is no indication that they will improve in the near future. The large unused capacity in the industry exerts pressure on prices. Firms which are aggressive in marketing probably earn a profit. Mergers and specialization should reduce future costs. Hence, no developing country should plan the manufacture of heavy electrical equipment on the assumption that the present world market prices are abnormally low and therefore unlikely to endure.

If world market prices are accepted as a proper standard for comparisons, the next question is how prices in the countries studied compare with world market prices. Such information has been derived in this study from analysis of prices quoted in international tenders supplemented by interviews with manufacturers. This comparison is valid only for categories of equipment which are both produced in the country and imported. The categories compared differ between countries, and the conclusions do not necessarily apply to equipment which is not presently imported. With these and other reservations, we found typical price differences of 25 to 60 percent for a range of items (1964 data). The difference tended to fall substantially and quite rapidly as more production experience was gained. Mexican transformer production provides a good illustration of this. Price differences were also very much influenced by the size of the domestic component, particularly in generators. In Spain, where the industry has reached considerable maturity, present domestic prices are probably no more than 20 to 25 percent above the international level. The price comparison was most favorable for medium-sized transformers and switchgear—these are items produced in relatively small numbers to individual design and they do not require very powerful manufacturing facilities.

In our discussions, we often encountered the argument that, even accepting that world market prices are going to remain low for a long period to come, it is incorrect to compare prices in developing countries with prices below average production costs in industrialized countries. Under a rational allocation of resources, there is no reason for protection other than infant industry protection; balance of payments equilibrium may be restored essentially through the exchange rate adjustment.[1] The fact that equipment is offered on the world market at prices below the average cost of production or even at subsidized prices is a bargain for purchasers. In this sense, it is no different from, say, a discovery of important new copper resources which would reduce the price of copper. The world market for copper has to be taken as given; there is no reason for exploiting uneconomic low-grade domestic deposits.

Present Cost Comparisons

We compare actual costs in Western Europe and in the countries studied, and then analyze actual costs in relation to theoretically attainable costs.

Major raw materials for heavy electrical equipment are considerably more expensive in the countries studied than in industrial countries. In a few cases, this reflects high duties on imported materials (e.g. transformer grade steel sheets in Brazil) or tied-aid procurement. In other cases, importers taking advantage of restricted supplies may charge high prices. Most often perhaps, material costs are high because of high prices charged by protected domestic industries (ordinary steel sheets, dynamo-grade steel sheets, semi-manufactures of copper). Often these high prices primarily reflect the high costs associated with infant industries; in many cases they also reflect various inefficiencies and monopoly profits.

Wages for comparable skills in 1965 were only about 40 percent of the German levels in Spain, about one-third of that level in Brazil, and about one-fifth in India. Differences in salaries were considerably less: in Brazil, wages for comparable skills were 32 percent of the German level while salaries were 62 percent of the corresponding level. On balance, the average cost per man-year will be considerably lower in developing countries. This could give them a competitive edge, since manpower costs in industrialized countries account for up to 40 percent of the selling price for heavy electrical equipment. Up to now this advantage has been offset by lower productivity. Our best evidence suggests that two to three times as many direct man-hours have been used in making heavy electrical equipment in Brazil or Mexico as in Western Europe. Since the proportion of indirect labor is high in developing countries, and ratios of staff to labor very similar to those in Western European plants, the lower productivity of direct labor also holds true for total manpower.

---

[1] It is obvious that in the case where one industry has a pronounced comparative advantage in relation to any other, such as oil in Libya or Venezuela, mere reliance on the exchange rate may kill off the other industries.

The above productivity figures should be interpreted cautiously. Their comparability is limited by differences in the composition of the labor force and different degrees of vertical integration. High labor productivity is not necessarily synonymous with economic efficiency; this would also depend upon the quantities of other factors used such as materials and capital.

In order to consider all cost factors, we use the following approach. First, we select manufacturers, both in Western Europe and in developing countries (specifically Spain and Brazil) who have specialized in the production of heavy electrical equipment. Secondly, we divide all costs into material costs, manpower costs, and charges against capital, and express each category as a ratio to sales. Thirdly, we deflate sales of the firms in the developing countries to Western European prices. This made it possible to express each one of the three cost elements, both for Western Europe and for the developing countries, as a ratio to sales valued at Western European prices and to compare these cost elements both singly and in terms of their total impact.

Our comparison suggests that manpower costs per dollar of sales at constant prices were 25 to 60 percent higher in Brazil and Mexico than in Western Europe, corresponding to a cost difference of about 10 cents for each dollar of sales. Charges against capital in developing countries were about twice the Western European level which makes a difference of about 13 cents for each dollar of sales. Under capital charges we include depreciation, interest, profits, and income taxes.

The final balance sheet of present cost comparisons indicated Spanish and Brazilian costs 40 to 45 percent above the Western European level. About 16 percent could be explained by higher prices for materials and components, 10 to 15 percent by higher manpower costs and 13 percent by higher charges against capital.

At the time our comparison was made and *under the conditions* in which the industry was then operating in Brazil, it would consequently have needed the following average protection to earn a 20 percent return on the total assets employed:

| | Industrial Country | | | Required Protection | |
	Home prices	Export	Brazil	Based on home prices	Based on export prices
				percent	percent
Raw materials and purchased components ("inputs")	51.5	51.5	67.3	30	30
Conversion margin	48.5	32.5	74.5	53	130
Final selling price f.o.b.	100.0	84	141.8	42	68
c.i.f. developing country		92	141.8		54

93

Only to a minor extent do the above cost differences reflect differences in productivity in a narrow sense. After the initial learning period, the operating times on the same production machines are virtually identical in Brazil and in Western Europe.

Nor would it be true to say that a large home market is a decisive condition for comparative advantage. Most of the countries studied have home markets as large as some very competitive Western European manufacturers. True economies of scale in the production of heavy electrical equipment are apparently quite modest. In other words, costs would not differ greatly between a plant with a capacity for making two very large generators over a given period, say 18 months, and a plant with a capacity for only one such item in the same period. What matters is that the plant should be well adjusted to the size and needs of the market, and that it should receive an even flow of orders.

The key to success in the manufacture of heavy electrical equipment would seem to lie in some combination of the following factors:

a) A gradual and efficient buildup of capacity, avoiding excessive diversification;

b) Government policies aiming at an even flow of orders for the local industry and preventing the multiplication of producers;

c) Efficient management, skillfully coordinating every aspect of production and sales;

d) Research and development, permitting good profits on advanced types of equipment where world market prices are relatively high.

In the latter area, developing countries have a comparative disadvantage which will not be overcome in the short run. The other three conditions, in our view, will be generally fulfilled to the extent that the technological and management know-how of international concerns are combined with a proper institutional framework in the developing country.

The Role of Protection

In most of the countries studied, the industry is already emerging from the infant stage, and is heavily protected. Progress has been reasonable but has fallen short of what was actually attainable in several of the countries studied. In retrospect, efficient growth might have been promoted by the following type of arrangement with an international manufacturer covering a specified infant industry period:

a) A detailed plan for the development of the industry during this period, including arrangements with power companies regarding domestic procurement;

b) Support by government during the infancy of the industry, but not thereafter.

In most of the countries studied there has probably been enough time for learning with respect to the types of equipment presently made. In practice, learning is a function of jobs done rather than time elapsed; an excessive number of producers and an uneven flow of work has lengthened this period in some countries. In order to encourage the growth of existing industries, some extension of protection during a period of adjustment might be defended. The corporations, for their part, should encourage manufacture in developing countries with the ultimate aim of achieving the optimum location of plants around the world.

ANNEX A

EXCHANGE RATE ADJUSTMENT IN ARGENTINA[1]

One of the most difficult methodological issues faced in our study was the dual problem of a) the exchange rates to be used in international price comparisons and b) the measurement of the actual rate of protection. As is shown below, with special reference to Argentina, these two issues, to an extent at least, are closely interrelated.

After the peso was devalued in 1958, prices continued to rise in Argentina, and the Government maintained balance in its external payments by introducing surcharges ("recargos") of 75 to 175 percent above normal tariffs. This system remained in force until March 13, 1967, when the peso was devalued from 190 pesos to 350 pesos to one US dollar with a simultaneous reduction in most tariff duties by about 40 percent.

The high level of surcharge prior to devaluation[2] clearly contained a large element of compensation for the overvalued exchange rate. We decided, for comparative and presentational purposes, to substitute for the existing combination of exchange rates, import duties (and export subsidies), a new combination of higher exchange rates, lower import duties (and new export taxes) which, in the end, would leave all prices in Argentine currency the same as before. *This would throw some light on the gross protection enjoyed by dif-*

---

[1] This note was contributed by Bertil Walstedt.

[2] This study was based on price and cost information from December 1965.

ferent industries. The key to this adjustment was the assumption that instead of an estimated average 108 percent duty on all imported articles,[3] the average import duty corresponding to legitimate needs for infant industry protection in a country at Argentina's stage of industrial development would be about 25 percent. This, of course, is essentially an arbitrary device to permit comparative protection to be judged. Any reader having reason to believe that some other figure (say, 35 or 10 percent) would be more reasonable could easily substitute his own assumption.

On this basis, the appropriate accounting rate as of December 1965 was computed as follows:

Nominal exchange rate	190	pesos
Average utilized protection (108%)	205	pesos
Exchange rate, integrating all duties	395	pesos
Exchange rate, integrating all duties except 25 percent average infant industry protection (395/1.25):	316	pesos

To avoid misunderstanding, two aspects of this adjustment may be spelled out. Conceptually, the increase in the exchange rate, in order to keep all export prices the same as before, should be accompanied by the introduction of export taxes. We are not suggesting this as a policy; we are only trying to determine what were the actual (as distinguished from the apparent) implications of the policies pursued. Or, viewing the problem from another angle, we are interested in the international competitiveness and the degree of protection enjoyed by the manufacturers of heavy electrical equipment in Argentina. For this purpose we needed a meaningful accounting rate for foreign exchange.

Secondly, we do not know whether the combination of exchange rates, tariff protection, and some quantitative restrictions in force in December 1965 was consistent with equilibrium in the supply and demand for foreign exchange, and whether, therefore, our calculated rate (with the attendant assumptions on import duties and subsidies) was an "equilibrium" rate. The most that can be claimed is a negative conclusion. There is no positive evidence that, assuming inflation had been stopped in December 1965, the then existing system would *not* have been consistent with the balance-of-payments equilibrium.

---

[3] The unweighted average duty (duties and surcharges consolidated) before devaluation was found to be 127 percent of which, on the average, domestic producers were thought to take advantage of only 108 percent protection.

ANNEX B

PRODUCTIVITY AND THE LEARNING
PROCESS – SOME ILLUSTRATIONS

Case I—Pakistan. Distribution Transformers and Motors

The following table shows actual productivities in the second and third year of operations compared with established productivity targets.

	Second Year	Third Year	Target
Production per sq. metre of production space per month	45	89	100
Production per man-month	59	70	100
Production per direct man-hour	42	59	100

In this plant, direct labor productivity was lagging, partly because of excessive labor turnover. By drawing in extra labor, total production was nevertheless kept relatively close to targets and deliveries were reasonably respected.

Case II—Argentina. Power Transformers

The total man-hours required in the production of transformers (of a reasonably stable product mix) by an Argentine plant fell by about 28 percent over a seven-year period:

Years	Man-hours per kva in Transformer Production
1958	1.63
1959	2.11
1960	1.59
1961	1.59
1962	1.52
1963	1.67
1964	1.38
1965	1.17

The figures for 1959 and 1963 deviate from the general trend; in these years there was a shortage of orders, and the production of the company dropped.

Case III—Brazil. Water Wheel Generators and Power Transformers

The following figures are somewhat more difficult to interpret since the composition of the output has changed and there have been changes in capacity utilization. Nevertheless, there is clearly a decrease in manpower requirements:

Man-hours per kva in the production of water wheel generators and transformers

	1962	1963	1964	1965
Water wheel generators (man-hours/kva)	–	9.0	1.5	4.4
Transformers (man-hours/kva)	1.2	0.5	0.7	0.9

Case IV—Mexico. Power Transformers

According to the official quotations, the price changes are as follows:

Transformer prices in $ per kva

	1957	1961–62	1964
5 Mva		7.66	4.03
10–12 Mva		4.95	2.70
20 Mva	3.50[a]	4.14	2.00

[a] Roughly extrapolated from the first two observations in the data. The transformers used as illustrations are comparable in terms of total power rating but not necessarily in other characteristics. Hence, they give only a rough indication of the price trend.

Annex Table 17 suggests that the ratio of Mexican prices to the lowest foreign bid fell from a typical range of 1.25 to 1.6 times the *c.i.f.* price of foreign equipment in 1957–1960 to 0.9 to 1.1 times that price in 1964. Besides the element of learning on the Mexican side, the shrinking of the differences may also reflect reduced protection and increased needs for business by the Mexican producer.

ANNEX TABLES

ANNEX TABLE 1: Heavy Electrical Equipment Manufacturers: Structure of Assets and Liabilities, 1964

(percent of total assets)

	ASEA, Sweden	Brown Boveri, Germany	ACEC, Belgium	CEM, France	General Electrica Española, Spain	Brown Boveri, Brazil
Fixed assets	15.9	20.8	13.5	16.4	35.2	37.5
Investments	24.6	13.8	9.3	5.8	–	–
Current assets	59.5	63.3	77.2	77.8	64.8	62.5
Other assets	–	2.1	–	–	–	–
Gross assets	100.0	100.0	100.0	100.0	100.0	100.0
Equity	55.5	49.0	35.9	15.8	48.9	43.9
Long-term debt	13.5	6.0	15.7	12.7	11.7	0.5
Current liabilities	31.0	37.3	48.4	71.5	39.4	55.6
Other liabilities	–	7.7	–	–	–	–
Gross liabilities	100.0	100.0	100.0	100.0	100.0	100.0
Gross assets (US $ million)	255.0	211.5	127.8	94.5	55.7	10.2
Total sales (US $ million)	195.0[a]	263.8[a]	126.7	109.0	41.7	7.9
Ratio gross assets/sales[b]	1.31	0.80	1.01	0.87	1.33	1.29

[a] Parent company only.
[b] Including investments under assets.

ANNEX TABLE 2: Export and Import of Heavy Electrical Equipment, 1965

($'000)

	Electrical Power Machinery	Switchgear	Elec. Furnaces Elec. Welding and Cutting Apparatus	Electric Condensers (Capacitors)	Total
S.I.T.C.	722	723	729.9 (2)	729.9 (5)	
USA					
Import	39,137	28,049	12,260*	15,541*	94,987
Export	270,639	201,835	103,250*	21,859*	597,583
Canada					
Import	58,660	55,689	2,613	–	116,962
Export	16,232	11,278	599*ᵃ	–	28,109
Austria					
Import	13,825	17,819	2,274*	3,016*	36,934
Export	21,406	12,132	3,536*	1,590*	38,664
Belgium-Luxembourg					
Import	38,010	44,683	7,044†	9,592†	99,329
Export	34,154	24,047	8,245†	4,071†	70,517
France					
Import	33,987	53,879	12,816*	9,204*	109,886
Export	77,150	86,606	11,968†	5,115*	180,839
Italy					
Import	28,272	37,873	5,504*	15,605*	87,254
Export	36,351	41,186	10,039*	7,032*	94,608
Germany, Federal					
Import	49,076	68,527	11,985†	9,049†	138,637
Export	188,116	212,316	45,604†	21,746†	467,782
Holland					
Import	65,569	60,320	6,407†	16,101†	148,397
Export	37,534	36,511	7,599†	16,485†	98,129
Sweden					
Import	32,982	44,658	4,491*	5,836*	87,877
Export	40,952	17,495	7,352*	3,669*	69,468
Switzerland					
Import	22,999	23,248	3,877*	3,221*	53,345
Export	36,677	46,680	12,617*	2,644*	101,618
UK					
Import	31,677	56,181	11,050*	7,636*	106,544
Export	139,006	104,017	18,262*	7,465	268,750

	Electrical Power Machinery	Switchgear	Elec. Furnaces Elec. Welding and Cutting Apparatus	Electric Condensers (Capacitors)	Total
S.I.T.C.	722	723	729.9 (2)	729.9 (5)	
Japan					
Import	17,717	16,968	6.612*	742*	42,039
Export	63,131	37,167	6,811*	20,493	127,602
Spain					
Import	32,270	21,719	5,886	2,783	62,658
Export	2,528	1,617	555	279	4,979
Mexico					
Import	23,617	19,401	3,001*	1,214	47,233
Export	–	–	17	–	17
Argentina					
Import	91,162*	430*	–	–	91,592
Export	–	–	–	–	–
Brazil					
Import	6,319	14,167	1,127*b	1,725*b	23,338
Export	–	–	13*b	94*b	107
India					
Import	84,609	9,396*c	4,032*c	95*c	98,132
Export	–	45*	–	–	45
Pakistan					
Import	–	–	809*d	173*d	982
Export	–	–	5d	–	5

a Industrial furnaces only.
b Figure for year 1964, Brazil National Statistics.
c Year from April 1964–March 1965.
d Figure for July 1965–June 1966, Pakistan Monthly Trade Statistics.
* National Statistics.
† Statistical Office of the EEC, *Foreign Trade.*
Source: UN, *Commodity Trade Statistics.*
Note: The figures on trade in electrical machinery for 1965 must be read with great care. As far as possible we have tried to maintain comparability between countries. However, in no case were we able to separate heavy equipment from light equipment; thus the figures presented are for all sizes and weights of equipment in a given class. Moreover, the breakdown of electrical equipment into classes varied in detail. Therefore, figures for a class for one country may be more precise than for another. As much information as was available was taken from UN or EEC sources where the classification system is the same as the one shown here. For more information, it was ultimately necessary to go to the statistics published by the individual countries, with resulting problems in reclassification.

ANNEX TABLE 3: Degrees of Self-Sufficiency in the Production of Electric Power Machinery and Switchgear, 1965

(percent)

	Production/Consumption	Export/Production	Import/Consumption
United States	112	12	2
Germany	127	35	11
United Kingdom	117	22	10
France	119	34	22
Italy	109[b]	61	57
Sweden[a]	90	32	39
Belgium[a]	86	37	46
Netherlands[a]	54	121[d]	112[d]
India[a]	28	–	72
Spain[a]	58	6	46
Brazil[a]	67[c]	4	33
Austria[a]	104	63	62
Argentina	77[c]	–	22
Pakistan	18	–	82

[a] In these cases earlier production figures were combined with 1965 trade figures if later production figures were not available. This is true of Belgium (1963), Netherlands (1964), India (1961), Spain (1964), Brazil (1964), Austria (1964), and Sweden (1964).

[b] The production share of this figure covers all switchgear but only rotating electric plant in the power machinery category.

[c] Power machinery only, excluding switchgear.

[d] The Netherlands imports individual items which are re-exported as part of larger equipment.

Note: Trade figures covering the entire class 722 in the SITC classification are generally taken from UN publications. While every attempt has been made to fit national production statistics to this classification, the results, at best, can be only approximations.

ANNEX TABLE 4: Maximum Specifications of Units Manufactured or in the Process of Manufacture, by Countries, January 1, 1967

	Thermal Generators (MW)	Hydraulic Generators (MW)	Power Transformers (Mva)	Nuclear Reactors (MWe)
Austria	210	102	660	–
Belgium	325	142	660	600
Denmark	10[a]	10	240	–
France	600	230	700	500
Germany	345	160	1,000	383
Italy	380	150	380	–
Netherlands	131	10	237	–
Norway	–	242	448	–
Portugal	–	–	150	–
Spain	40	81	200	–
Sweden	275	200	700[b]	420
Switzerland	500	115	333	–
United Kingdom	660	143	750	600

[a] Diesel generator.
[b] Three phase units, 400 kv.
Source: Nineteenth and Twentieth Surveys of Electrical Power Equipment, OECD, Paris.

ANNEX TABLE 5: Importance of Different Materials in Cost Structure for Power Transformers and Heavy Motors, Mexico, 1966

(total ex-factory cost = 100)

	Copper	Silicon Steel Sheets	Carbon Steel Sheets, etc.	Insulating Materials	Oil	Bushings	Others	All Materials
Transformers								
125 Mva—115/6.6 kv	15.8	21.2	6.0	3.9	5.9	6.6	17.5	76.9
25/33 Mva—161/60 kv	18.6	24.0	4.6	4.3	5.3	8.7	11.4	76.9
40/55.3 Mva—115/6.6/13.8 kv	10.1	22.6	3.0	2.7	0.8	5.4	32.4	76.9
92 Mva—220/13.2 kv	11.9	30.4	3.6	3.4	0.6	6.9	20.2	76.9
Motors								
50 hp 3 phase induction motor								
50/60 cps. 220/440	12.16	20.86	5.25	3.20	–	–	22.52	64.0
200 hp horizontal motor 50/60 cycle								
220/440 v	12.7	27.7	7.9	3.2	–	–	14.70	66.2

Source: Interviews with individual companies, 1966.

ª Expressed in relation to the price to the user (including sales overhead and profits), these percentages would be considerably lower. See for instance the following table.

ANNEX TABLE 6: Cost Structure of a Generator, Argentina, 1965

(percent of sales price)

Material	22.4	
Steel sheets		4.7
Silicon steel		3.4
Copper		6.4
Steel arms		1.8
Insulation material		5.5
Ball-bearings		0.4
Other		0.2
Manpower	26.3	
Direct labor		11.4
Indirect labor		6.8
Social benefits, etc.		8.1
Overhead	37.8	
Services and maintenance		7.2
Operating supply		4.0
Royalties, licenses, etc.		3.7
Research		1.2
General manufacturing expenses		5.5
Legal expenses		2.4
Depreciation		2.2
Interest		6.2
Taxes		5.4
Sales and distribution expenses	3.5	
Profit	10.0	
Sales price	100.0	

Source: Interviews with companies, 1965.

ANNEX TABLE 7: Breakdown of Material Costs, Firms in Developing Countries, 1965

(total material cost = 100)

	Transformers			Motors		Generators
	230/13.2 kv 92 Mva	161/60 kv 25 Mva	115/6.6 kv 12.4 Mva	200 hp 220/440 v	50 hp 220/440 v	5 Mva
Silicon steel sheets	40.6	31.6	27.6	41.8	32.6	15.2
Copper	16.5	24.6	20.6	19.2	19.0	28.6
Carbon steel	5.8	6.0	7.9	11.8	8.2	21.1
Insulation material	5.6	5.7	5.1	4.9	5.0	24.3
Subtotal	68.5	67.9	61.2	77.7	64.8	89.2
Bushings, high voltage	9.5	9.9	7.3	–	–	–
Bushings, low voltage	0.5	1.6	1.3	–	–	–
Cooling elements	17.3	5.9	15.6	–	–	–
Oil	0.8	6.9	7.6	–	–	–
Castings	–	–	–	13.9	13.1	8.5[a]
Bearings	–	–	–	5.0	5.0	1.8
Subtotal	28.1	24.3	31.8	18.9	18.1	10.3
Others	3.4	7.8	7.0	3.4	17.1	0.5
Total	100.0	100.0	100.0	100.0	100.0	100.0

[a] This refers, in the case of generators, to steel arms.
Source: Interviews with companies.

ANNEX TABLE 8: **Inputs as percent of Total Material Cost, a Mexican Firm, 1964 and 1965, and a Pakistani Firm, 1965–66**

Mexican Firm	1964	1965	Pakistani Firm	1965–66
Copper products	27.9	27.8	Bought-in parts	41.9
Silicon steel	24.7	24.6	Iron and steel	25.5
Tape and insulation	7.6	7.6	Copper and brass	16.1
Transformer oil	7.1	7.0		
Black steel sheets	5.7	5.6	Subtotal	83.5
Subtotal	73.0	72.6	Chemicals and transformer oil	7.6
			Standard and auxiliary material	4.1
Tubes for radiators	5.0	4.9	Insulating material	3.2
Steel strip samples	2.0	2.0	Welding material	1.6
Welding bars	1.5	1.5		
Electric energy	1.4	1.4	Total	100.0
Switches	1.4	1.4		
Subtotal	11.3	11.2		
Varnish	1.0	1.0		
Thermometers	0.7	1.0		
Oxygen and acetylene	0.9	0.8		
Bushes	0.7	0.7		
Valves	0.5	0.5		
Subtotal	3.8	4.0		
Nuts and bolts	0.3	0.3		
Others	11.7	11.9		
Total	100.0	100.0		

Source: Interviews with individual firms, 1966.

ANNEX TABLE 9: Comparison of Direct Labor Requirements of Electrical Equipment, 1966[a]

Equipment		Man-hours Required in		Ratios
		Developing countries	Industrial countries[b]	
Small fractional motor	Mexico	5.4	1	5.4
Diesel generator 1500 kva; 90 rpm	Brazil	1,850	600	3.1
Transformer 33 kva—220/88 kv	Brazil	9,880	4,100	2.4
Water wheel generator 42 Mva—13820 v	Brazil	28,000	16,000	1.75

[a] The above comparison refers only to the labor required in the factory; it does not take into account the differences in design work and in sales. Nor does it weigh the effect of different skill requirements resulting from different manufacturing techniques.

[b] United States, Federal Republic of Germany, and Sweden.

Source: Interviews with individual companies, 1966.

112

ANNEX TABLE 10: Manpower Costs in the Manufacture of Heavy Electrical Equipment, Related to Sales and Value Added, Industrial and Developing Countries, 1964

	Average Wages per Hour	Average Salaries per Month	Ratio of Salary Earners to Wage-Earners	Payroll per Man Employed per Year ($)	Sales per Man Employed ($)	Value Added per Man Employed ($)
USA[a]	4.63	696	1/2.6	6,250	19,350	11,200
France[b]	1.22	424	1/1.9	2,920	10,900	5,420
Argentina[c]	0.88	157[g]	1/2.0	1,474	2,928	1,747
Brazil[d]	0.52	165	1/1.6	1,980	6,930	2,730
Mexico[e]	0.74	355	1/2.0	1,690	5,600	3,060
Spain	0.85	150	1/2.0	2,180	6,290	2,600
Pakistan[f]	0.24	102	1/3.8	950	5,600	2,700

[a] Based on 1963 Census of Manufacturing Industry which covers the manufacture of transformers, switchgear and rotating machines.

[b] Calculated on the basis of Rapport Statistique, 1965; Syndicat Général de la Construction Electrique.

[c] CEGELEC, CEE, Siam, Electromecanica and EMA, 1964. Exchange rate used: 262 pesos per US $1 instead of the average official rate for the year 1964 which was 138 pesos. The rate used for 1964 was based on an assumed parity rate of 316 pesos for 1965 adjusted backwards by means of the wholesale price index.

[d] Brown Boveri S.A., 1964. The other major producer, GE, was still in the process of starting up operations.

[e] Average calculated on the basis of IEM, IESA, 1964 and GE,, 1965.

[f] Average of Pakelektron, Climax, Johnson and Phillips, and Siemens, 1964–1965.

[g] Rough approximation since the average social charges on salaries are not known.

113

ANNEX TABLE 11: Price Assumptions for the Analysis in Chapter VI

	Argentina	Brazil	Mexico	Spain	India	Pakistan
a. World market price, *c.i.f.*	100	100	100	100	100	100
b. Domestic price	140	130	145	125	160	130
c. French export price, *f.o.b.*	92	92	92	95	92	92
d. French domestic price	110	110	110	110	110	110
ratio b/d, percent	127	118	133	114	145	118

ANNEX TABLE 12: Examples of the Calculation of Price Levels

	Output	Corresponding Cost if Imported	Price Ratio
	(1)	(2)	(1) ÷ (2)
Brazil	(*US $'000*)		
Transformers	8,620	6,360	1.35
Generators	536	357	1.50
Motors and others	5,280	4,220	1.25
General relative price	14,436	10,937	1.31
Pakistan	(*Rs '000*)		
Transformers	19,279	16,000	1.20
Motors	13,643	9,620	1.42
Switchgear	10,968	8,100	1.35
General relative price	42,880	33,720	1.27

ANNEX TABLE 13: **Composition of Gross Profits, Profit-to-Sales and Sales to Assets Ratios for Representative European Manufacturers of Heavy Electrical Equipment**

(millions of currency named)

	ASEA, Sweden, SwKr (1964)	ACEC, Belgium, US $ (1964)	CEM, France, Frs (1965)
1. Depreciation	32.0	3.5	20.9
2. Interest	7.7	1.3	7.1
3. Taxes	64.0	0.7	4.5
4. Net profits	102.1	2.2	0.5ᵇ
Gross profits			
5. Total	205.8	7.7	64.1ᶜ
6. From sales	162.6	7.0	61.7
7. Other	43.2	0.7	2.4
Turnover			
8. Total	1,054.0	126.7	545.0
9. Sales	1,011.8	126.0	542.0
Assets			
10. Total	1,319.2	147.9	464.9
11. Net of advances, subsidiaries, and trade investments	1,070.0ᵃ	136.0ᵃ	433.8ᵃ
Ratios, percent			
12. (6) to (9), profits from sales to sales	16.0	5.6	9.6ᶜ
13. (5) to (8), gross profits to turnover	19.5	6.1	9.9ᶜ
14. (11) to (9), net assets to sales	100.0	108.0	80.0ᵈ
15. (5) to (10), gross profits to assets	16.2	5.2	14.2

ᵃ Excluding advances to subsidiary companies and others and shares in subsidiary companies and others from assets.

ᵇ Adding Frs. 2.8 million shown as a "depreciation on shares and other investments."

ᶜ Including "Allocation from the current operating year to various contingency reserves" (comptes de prévision).

ᵈ After deducting turnover taxes and payroll taxes from total sales.

ANNEX TABLE 14: Production of Transformers by Manufacturer, India, 1962

Name of Firm	Above 2000 kva		1000–2000 kva		750–1000 kva		500–750 kva	
	Nos.	kva	Nos.	kva	Nos.	kva	Nos.	kva
Hackbridge-Hewittic & Easun Ltd., Bombay	38	189,450	6	14,200	22	17,800	25	18,410
National Electric Industries, Bombay	18	98,000	42	68,000	36	38,550	31	22,495
Crompton Parkinson (Works) Ltd., Bombay	22	87,500	37	58,050	37	37,800	42	30,300
Transformer & Switch-gear Ltd., Madras	15	49,000	..	..	11	11,000	..	..
AEI, Calcutta	6	17,200	8	13,550	21	19,800	11	8,100
Kirloskar Electric Co., Bangalore	3	15,000	19	26,450	16	16,000	17	12,300
Electric Construction & Equipment Co., Calcutta	5	10,000	2	2,750	19	19,500	39	28,850
Bharat Bijlee Ltd., Bombay	..	..	4	5,850	28	29,200	2	1,560
General Electric Co., Calcutta	..	..	11	22,400	17	16,774	17	12,450
Ghandi Electric Industries, Bombay	..	..	2	3,000	2	2,000	28	20,760
Hindustan Elec. Co., Baroda	..	..	..	1,000	1	1,000	2	1,500
Government Elec. Factory, Bangalore	..	..	1	1,500	4	4,000	1	600
Radio & Electls. Ltd., Madras	..	..	..	..	..	..	1	750
Bajaj Electl. Ltd., Bombay	..	..	..	..	..	..	..	..
Andhra Pradesh Electric Equipment Corp., Visakhapatnam	..	..	..	..	..	..	..	..
Indian Transformers, Alwaye	..	..	..	..	..	..	..	..
Pradip Lamp Works, Patna	..	..	..	..	..	..	..	..
Total	107	466,150	132	215,750	214	213,424	216	158,075
Percent		(20.3)		(9.4)		(9.3)		(6.9)

250–500 kva		75–250 kva		25–75 kva		Up to 25 kva		Total	
Nos.	kva	Nos.	kva	Nos.	kva	Nos.	kva	Nos.	kva
15	5,450	391	43,050	601	36,800	155	3,950	1,253	329,110
94	42,550	205	38,100	123	5,845	111	2,775	660	316,315
137	60,200	474	67,715	102	4,578	742	13,552	1,593	359,695
1	500	32	3,400	352	18,900	..	..	411	82,800
49	24,150	32	6,650	16	848	2	30	145	90,328
101	45,050	966	125,450	104	5,425	4	81	1,230	245,756
94	40,800	736	80,350	326	16,350	1,503	37,610	2,724	236,210
38	16,800	105	19,750	432	20,625	577	13,175	1,186	106,960
165	65,423	224	36,750	534	21,155	627	10,110	1,595	184,862
31	13,650	153	22,470	21	1,014	1	25	238	62,919
9	3,900	75	8,350	33	2,230	1	25	121	17,005
46	21,700	384	58,010	194	9,695	744	14,760	1,404	110,265
17	8,500	142	15,850	128	6,250	..	..	288	31,350
64	26,500	314	48,975	95	4,775	..	..	473	80,250
..	..	100	10,000	275	14,250	202	5,175	577	29,425
..	..	3	300	164	8,200	37	925	204	9,425
..	..	..	..	105	3,200	..	..	105	3,200
861	375,173 (16.3)	4,336	584,970 (25.5)	3,605	180,140 (7.9)	4,736	102,193 (4.4)	14,207	2,295,875 (100)

ANNEX TABLE 15: Price Comparison of Transformers in Mexico: Prices Quoted by Different Companies for the Same Job

(Mexican manufacturers' price = 100)

Item	Transformer	Mexico	Austria	France	Germany	Italy	Sweden	Switzer-land	UK	USA	Japan
1957											
1	Transformers 18.5/24 Mva—110/44/13.2 kv	100	56	73	–	64	–	77	–	94	–
2	Transformers 16/22 Mva—110/13.2 kv	100	95	80	–	77	–	96	134	–	–
3	Transformers 25 Mva—115/13.2 kv	100	93	118	–	66	118	103	–	112	134
4	Transformers 18 Mva—110/69 kv	100	63	77	–	75	–	82	–	115	–
1958											
1	Transformers 33/44 Mva—220/13.2 kv	100	–	94	134	91	–	99	–	151	98
1960											
1	Transformers 25 kva—115/13.2 kv	100	–	–	–	60	–	–	–	–	–
2	Case 2. Transformers 20 kva	100	–	–	–	–	–	60	–	–	–

118

1961										
1 Transformers 30 Mva—154/13.8 kv	100	–	–	–	52	–	80	–	–	62
2 Transformers 30 Mva—154/69 kv	100	94	–	–	76	–	106	–	–	–
3 Transformers 8 Mva—106/6 kv	100	–	–	–	76	–	73	–	–	–
1962										
1 Transformers 30/40 Mva—110/13.8 kv	100	–	–	–	74	–	91	112	73	65
2 Transformers 15/20 Mva—138/13.8 kv	100	–	63	–	–	–	92	94	72	45
3 Auto 35 Mva—138/69 kv	100	–	–	–	93	–	138	128	82	68
4 Case 4	100	–	–	–	76	–	106	130	85	61

Note: The underlined offer is the lowest offer.
Source: Review of international bids in Mexico.

ANNEX TABLE 16: Price Indices for Mexican Large Motors Compared to Imports, 1966

Three-phase, 4 Pole, 2280 rpm, Motors	Imported Motor						Domestic Motor		
								Domestic price	
	Price f.o.b. exporter	Freight, insurance	Handling charges	Duties	Commission to customs broker	Total landed cost incl. duty	Import f.o.b. = 100	Import c.i.f. = 100	Import Landed price = 100
Vertical									
75 hp	100	3.70	1.84	10.15	1.17	116.9	131	123	111
100 hp	100	3.67	1.67	10.15	1.14	116.6	158	151	135
125 hp	100	4.17	1.53	10.15	1.12	116.9	151	141	128
100 hp	100	3.95	1.35	10.15	1.12	116.6	161	155	125
200 hp	100	4.05	1.08	10.15	0.84	116.1	151	143	129
Average								143	
Horizontal									
75 hp	100	5.93	2.76	12.7	1.24	122.6	138	127	112
100 hp	100	5.17	2.18	11.2	1.13	119.7	144	134	120
125 hp	100	5.20	2.08	11.5	1.06	119.9	163	146	130
150 hp	100	4.30	1.72	10.0	1.00	117.0	165	144	130
200 hp	100	4.47	1.58	10.0	.90	116.9	161	152	137
Average								141	

Source: Interviews with firms.